Children's Stories

in

American Literature

1861–1896

by

Henrietta Christian Wright

NEW YORK

CHARLES SCRIBNER'S SONS

1899

TROW DIRECTORY
PRINTING AND BOOKBINDING COMPANY
NEW YORK

CHILDREN'S STORIES

IN

AMERICAN LITERATURE

SCRIBNER'S SERIES OF SCHOOL READING.

In Uniform Binding; each 12mo, net, 60 Cents.

THE CABLE STORY BOOK. Selections for School Reading, with the Story of the Author's Life. Edited by Mary E. Burt and Lucy Leffingwell Cable. Illustrated.

THE EUGENE FIELD BOOK. Verses, Stories, and Letters for School Reading. Edited by Mary E. Burt and Mary B. Cable. Introduction by George W. Cable. Illustrated.

FANCIFUL TALES. By Frank R. Stockton. Edited by Julia E. Langworthy. Introduction by Mary E. Burt.

THE HOOSIER SCHOOL-BOY. By Edward Eggleston. Illustrated.

CHILDREN'S STORIES IN AMERICAN LITERATURE, 1660–1860. By Henrietta C. Wright.

CHILDREN'S STORIES IN AMERICAN LITERATURE, 1860–1896. By Henrietta C. Wright.

ODYSSEUS, THE HERO OF ITHACA. By Mary E. Burt. A Translation of the Story of Odysseus as used in the Schools of Athens and Berlin. Fully Illustrated.

POEMS OF AMERICAN PATRIOTISM. Chosen by Brander Matthews. 285 pages.

TWELVE NAVAL CAPTAINS. By Molly Elliot Seawell. 233 pages. Illustrated.

CHAPTER I

GEORGE WILLIAM CURTIS

1824-1892

In a certain American classic there is a picture of a boy standing in the shadow of an old warehouse and living, in imagination, a day that belonged to another generation. The boy was George William Curtis, and it was in his charming book, *Prue and I*, that he embodied this experience of his boyhood. In the pages which describe the past glories of Providence the author is picturing his native city, and reproducing with an artist's touch the atmosphere which surrounded his childish days.

At that time Providence was sharing the fate of many New England seaport towns whose importance was passing away. The old, red, steep-roofed brick storehouses were

1

falling into ruins, the docks were crumbling away, and the business part of the town was almost deserted. In place of a fleet of great East India merchant-vessels moored to the big posts, there were only a few insignificant sloops idly rocking with the tides. Instead of the shouting and confusion of unlading, there was but a group of idle old sailors gathered in the warehouse doors.

But to the boy-dreamer who looked on, the silence and shadow of the old stores seemed like those of royal treasure-houses. There were still to be seen piles of East India wares —oriental stuffs, dyes, coffees, and spices whose fragrance brought Arabia and China to the senses. Occasionally a chance ship drifted into the harbor, and for a few hours the Providence wharves lived their old life. Once when this happened, young Curtis crept along the edge of the dock after the unloading was over, and at great risk leaned over and placed his hand against the black hulk. And thus, he records, he "touched Asia, Cape of Good Hope, and the Happy Islands; saw palm-groves, jungles, and Bengal tigers, and the feet of Chinese fairies."

From the gloom of the old warehouses he would very often go to the sunny fields that lay upon the hills back of the town, and watch some sea-bound ship, taking it for a type of his fortunes, which should sail "stately and successful to all the glorious ports of the future." The picture is bright and beautiful with the pure hopes of youth. It is good to know that the dream of the boy was a prophecy of the noble life it realized.

Providence was the home of young Curtis until his sixth year, when, with his elder brother, Burrill, he went for a time to school at Jamaica Plain, near Boston. From some fragments of description written many years afterward we learn that this experience was a pleasant one. The school was provided with large playgrounds, play-hours were long and study-hours short. Near by was a pond for boating and fishing, and beyond the village were groves for nutting and picnics. The master's wife always took tea with the boys, and the master himself was a good-natured man with a great fondness for playing practical jokes. Once when he knocked at the dormitory door during an exciting pillow-fight, the boys turned the joke upon him by putting out the lights, and, pretending that they thought him one of their schoolmates, pounded him so unmercifully that he was glad to rush from the room.

But there were serious moments, too, in life. In one of these Curtis, then about seven, arrayed himself in ministerial garb and solemnly preached a sermon, from the landing of the stairs, upon the consequences of evil-doing. Perhaps it was from the text of this sermon that he a little later wrote a treatise on murder, which, he said, always started with Sabbath-breaking; the Sabbath-breaker became in turn a user of profane language, then a thief, and so went downward by easy gradations until he committed murder. Such grave subjects, however, only occasionally depressed the spirits of this happy flock of boys. Curtis said that possibly they did not learn anything at this school, but that they had plenty of good beef.

There was a very deep love and sympathy between the Curtis brothers, and their life at Jamaica Plain, and afterward when they returned to Providence, is reflected in the work of later years where the picture of the brother is sketched with a loving hand.

While they were still very young boys they heard in their school-room, at Providence, a lecture by Emerson, who was then beginning to be known as an essayist and lecturer. Into these hearts, which had just left childhood, the words of Emerson fell full of gracious inspiration. He became their teacher of noble thoughts, their leader into the realm of moral beauty. Much as the page of chivalric days looked up to his chosen knight, they revered with boyish hero-worship the great teacher. He gave them the best things that Puritanism could bestow, and he became a far-reaching influence in their lives.

The Curtis family removed to New York in 1839, and the Providence school-days came to an end. But above all others Curtis always called Emerson his teacher; another tribute to the master to whom American thought owes so much.

The new home was in Washington Square, then the upper part of the city, with the open country not far away. The best-known people of the day—writers, artists, musicians, lovers of all art—found their way to the Curtis home. This companionship, together with systematic study, fostered rapid intellectual growth ; the boys made progress, but city life did not entirely please them. About this time the Community of Brook Farm was founded by the men destined to be among the intellectual leaders of America. Every member was pledged to help with the manual labor, and to contribute his share toward the intellectual life. It was a dream of the old Utopia, where life was simple and happiness abounded. The Curtis brothers begged their father to let them go and share this ideal home, and he consented. Although they went as boarders and did not become actual members of the community, its life was theirs. Here, where Emerson, Hawthorne, and Dana ploughed and hoed and planted, the two boys did their share. They drove cows, raked hay, and pulled weeds in the morning; in the afternoon they studied German, chemistry, and music; in the evening they danced or sang, had theatrical representations or talked philosophy.

Young Curtis absorbed the healthy atmosphere of this unconventional yet inspiring life, as he breathed the air from the dewy meadows and wild-rose hedges. It was a part of the hope and aspiration of youth brought down to actual touch, and he formed here more than one abiding and uplifting friendship.

The charm of the life did not quite dissolve when the brothers returned to New York, for within a few months they were again in the country as inmates of a farmhouse near Concord. Here they did farm work, made their own beds, cultivated a little garden, joined a club of which Emerson and Hawthorne were members, and, in fact, lived and did quite as they pleased. It was camp life with some of the discomforts left out and some privileges added, and it was an idyllic existence for a

youth who did not know just what he should
make of life, but who had determined that he
would make of it something noble.

While at Concord Curtis wrote two charming little stories that may be called a prelude
to his literary career. One of these tales is
that of the strange sights seen by a little girl
who possesses a pair of magic spectacles. It
is full of the poetic grace of a genuine folk-
story. In the chapter on Titbottom's Spectacles in *Prue and I*, the same *motif* is used.
Neither of the stories has ever been published.

His career was still undecided when, in his
twenty-second year, Curtis sailed for Europe
and a trip to the East. Although calling no
college his Alma Mater he was still the representative cultivated young American of his day.
He was well read in the German, Italian, and
English classics, appreciated the best music,
was a student of æsthetics, and had an earnest
and intelligent interest in politics. He believed that America, as embodying the idea of
self-government of states, had a mission to the
world. In his soul he consecrated his best

powers to the service of humanity, and he was ready, when the moment came, to serve it without thought of cost to himself. The ocean travellers of those days took passage in packet-ships, and Curtis was forty-six days in crossing to France. He spent four years abroad, making the usual tours. He kept a diary, which became a record of charming interest, but most of which remained unpublished. During this time he sent letters to the *New York Tribune*, devoted to the public questions of the day. The fact that he chose to write thus, while surrounded by the Old World impressions, shows the trend of his mind toward the higher political interests in which he became a leader.

During this trip Curtis seems to have made up his mind to a literary career. Soon after his return he began to lecture, and a little later went on the staff of the *Tribune. The Nile Notes of a Howadji* is the record of a trip up the Nile, and was the first book that Curtis published. Like Longfellow's *Hyperion*, it has more than a literary value as being the actual experience of one who was to become prominent in American literature. In these chapters the author did not aim at literal description. He was rather the happy traveller transcribing for absent friends the pictures of the lands they have so often visited together in imagination.

He made himself story-teller to the fireside group, and scene after scene was sketched with faithful hand. To this young dreamer Egypt still remained the land of wonder and inspiration, though its temples lay in ruins and its people had sunk to the lowest level of humanity. There is a wondrous charm in his sympathy with that great past, and in his appreciation of the ideals of the race whose art and science laid their mark ineffaceably upon the world. The paintings in the pyramids and tombs of the common people, illustrating the victories of the kings, the occupations of the lower classes, and even the games of the children, all pictured in colors still fresh, had a wonderful fascination for the young traveller. In gazing at them he forgot the Egypt that he actually saw and seemed to touch hands with a vanished race.

It throws a bright light on the character of the author to see him thus able to make that old inspiration his own. Without the *Nile Notes* we should never have known so well the ambitions of his young manhood when he was a dreamer of dreams. The chapters on the every-day occurrences of the trips are also full of interest, and touched with the author's characteristic humor.

The natives called all travellers howadji— shopkeepers — for such they conceived to be the occupation of the wandering Europeans and Americans who visited their land. To the native imagination the howadji was a being created to bestow bakshish, or alms, to buy bits of mummy bones, or even whole mummies, and to be cheated upon every occasion. Curtis refused to be cheated, gave bakshish only to the "miserable, old, and blind," and struck his followers dumb by insisting upon doing nothing for long hours but sit gazing upon a pyramid or ruined temple.

The journey up and down the Nile occupied two months, and the record of it will always be interesting as embodying the experiences of the Nile traveller in 1848. The literary charm of the book is great, many of the passages being in reality unrhymed poems of peculiar beauty. This volume was published in the spring of 1851, and was well received. There was an English edition which received many flattering notices, and this success confirmed the author in his determination to make literature his profession.

Mr. Curtis's next book, *A Howadji in Syria*, continued his journeyings in the East through Syria and Palestine. It is written in the style of the earlier work, and partakes of the same charm.

His third book, *Lotus-Eating*, had originally appeared in the *Tribune* as a series of letters written during a summer's journeyings through the Berkshire Hills, at Newport, and other sea-coast places, and at Niagara. This book is in Curtis's most delicate vein. *Lotus-Eating* was illustrated by Kensett, one of the

most popular artists of the day, and a warm
friend of the author. Both text and drawings
recall to-day the grace and beauty of some old
miniature in its quaint setting, a reflection of
another and more picturesque age.

The *Potiphar Papers* followed *Lotus-Eating*, and showed Curtis in the light of a
teacher of manners and morals to what was
called the best society. The Potiphar family
was a picture of the rich American without
cultivation, and with no other ambition than to
live in finer houses, have better horses, and
give more expensive dinners than the rest of
the world. In a series of letters by Mr. and
Mrs. Potiphar and their friends the author
shows the folly of such silly ambitions.

But the book which brought Mr. Curtis the
most fame, both because of its artistic excellence and high literary value, is that charming idyll, *Prue and I.* In these pages the
hero is an old book-keeper who lives in a
humble way in an unfashionable street. But
the book-keeper counts himself rich because
of his many castles in Spain, whither he often

travels, and about which he writes many delightful descriptions. There are other characters in the book who also own castles in
Spain. Titbottom, the under-book-keeper, and
Bourne, the millionnaire, share and share alike
in this wonderful property, which one is never
too poor to own, and never too rich not to desire. Each one tells stories in which Moorish
palaces, marble fountains, moonlit balconies,
West Indian sunsets, and tropical flowers are
woven into an arabesque of color; but somehow all suggest a dreamy-eyed boy lying upon
a sunny hill-slope watching an East Indian
merchantman sail out of Providence harbor
and fade away into a dim horizon.

There is one sweet and touching chapter
called "My Cousin the Curate," in which Curtis pays loving tribute to the character of his
brother Burrill. In the pages "Sea from
Shore" is found that charming description of
Providence in his youth, and "The Flying
Dutchman" is the immortal legend transformed anew. Throughout the book are
many pictures of the New York of forty years

ago ; what was then fashionable in manner, dress, and appointment ; the favorite actor, the most popular opera, the newest book, all are gossiped about by the old book-keeper who looks on. The descriptions, with their quaint fancies and poetic rendering, are alike rich in retrospective value.

Both the *Potiphar Papers* and *Prue and I* appeared first serially in *Putnam's Monthly*, of which Curtis was for a time associate editor. Five years after the publication of his first book Mr. Curtis took a position on *Harper's Magazine*, and inaugurated the Easy Chair. These delightful papers, which now are collected in several volumes, included criticisms on art, literature, music, social events, and similar topics, and were a never-ending source of interest and delight to his audience. Like that of Holmes, in the *Atlantic*, it was a purely literary office, and it showed, as no other review could, the wide intellectual sympathy of the editor. The Easy Chair was conducted for thirty-eight years by Mr. Curtis, being discontinued at his death.

In 1863 Curtis accepted the position of editor of *Harper's Weekly*. Perhaps no other American writer has ever been in such peculiar touch with the people as was the editor of the *Weekly* at this time. It was not a purely literary sympathy, for from the beginning his interest in public questions was reflected in the editorial page. Whatever vexing problem faced Congress, whatever measure in relation to government or reform was before the people, was used as a text by the lay preacher of the *Weekly*. The most unbounded respect was his, even from those whose opinion differed from his own, while his admirers learned to wait for the cool judgment and the wise word which never failed. Mr. Curtis was a strong friend of the anti-slavery cause, and both before and during the war he unflinchingly advocated its rights, though his course cost him more than one personal friend. During this period as a lecturer and delegate to conventions he reflected the creed of the national party. He was nominated for Congress and accepted the nomination, though he anticipated the defeat that awaited him in a State where his party was weak. Throughout the entire struggle he stood side by side with the great reformers, one of the most interesting figures of that stormy period.

Perhaps the public movement with which Mr. Curtis's name will remain most closely associated is the Civil Service Reform Commission, of which he was the first president and always the leading spirit. The object of this commission was to obtain legal power to advance all Government clerks and employees by regular promotions, in place of the political patronage which then obtained. This campaign for purer public service was begun in 1871, and from that time Mr. Curtis's work for it was unceasing, until the hopes of the reformers were fulfilled by the passage of the Civil Service Reform Law, which led the way in time to the needed reform.

From the beginning of his literary career Mr. Curtis had been known as a lecturer of singular power. His lectures embraced a wide variety of subjects, some of the most famous being

2

those delivered before colleges and at the meetings of the Chamber of Commerce in New York. Seventeen of these addresses alone were devoted to the civil service reform cause. His orations on the "Reunion of the Army of the Potomac;" on "Wendell Phillips;" "James Russell Lowell;" "Burns;" "The Puritan Principle;" "The Duty of the American Citizen to Politics," and other varied topics indicate the wide scope of this work. The abiding affection which he had inspired in the people at large made him one of the favorite orators at many commemorations of national importance. His orations and addresses are collected in thirteen volumes, and, with the *Harper's Weekly* editorials, form a scholarly review of one of the most interesting periods of American history.

Mr. Curtis's home was on Staten Island, where he died, in 1893.

CHAPTER II

1825—

The first recollections of Richard Henry Stoddard, like those of so many of our American men of letters, are of the sea. He was born at Hingham, Mass., a little seaport town, where his ancestors had lived for generations, and whence his father, Captain Stoddard, sailed away in his ship one day never to return. Somewhere between New York and the coast of Norway the brave little brig in which Captain Stoddard had invested all his fortune went down. Perhaps it struck an iceberg, or in the darkness of the northern sea mists came into collision with another vessel; no one ever heard its fate, and the widow and fatherless children only knew that to them had come that bitter portion which the sea gives to so many of its followers. For the first few years of his life young Stoddard had hardly any settled home, his mother moving from place to place, whenever a chance of bettering her fortunes presented itself. For a year or two he was at his grandfather's house at Hingham, which was situated on a hill overlooking the ocean, and below which was the graveyard where generations of seafaring folk lay buried. Among the memories which shine out from these earliest years are those of the old church at Hingham, where he solemnly sat in the old-fashioned high-backed pew, and of the admiring friends who, perhaps, on that same Sunday afternoon, pressed round him while he gravely recited one of Watts's hymns or some other of the pieces of which he had store. There is also a remembrance of a trip to Boston in his grandfather's schooner, an adventurous voyage no doubt to the small seafarer. From Hingham he went to live in several other New England towns, never staying long in one place, and settling at last in Boston, from which place, in his tenth year, he removed to New York on his mother's second marriage.

In all his sojournings he had never been quite out of sight and sound of the sea, and it was from this teacher no doubt that he learned to be a worshipper of beauty. Years afterward, when he began to translate his thoughts and emotions into verse, we find much of it touched with that indefinable, haunting mystery which is found only in the poetry of sealovers. And this quality is no doubt a reminiscence of those childish impressions which sank into his mind and became a part of it.

Stoddard's life in New York was varied in experience, although he had for the first time a settled home. The family was poor, and Stoddard went to school or became a bread-winner alternately, as their fortunes ebbed or flowed. At the age of fifteen he found himself confronted with the fact that the boy who eats bread and butter sometimes has to help pay for it to the extent of all his small might, and young as he was even then, he had no notion of shirking his duty. He became first the office-boy to a firm of two young lawyers, who had few clients, but who, nevertheless, advised him to forget poetry and study law. He worked for a time in a newspaper office; then he became book-keeper in a factory. For three or four days he tried earnestly to become a blacksmith, and at last, after much shifting of scene, he settled in a foundry and learned the trade of iron-moulding.

But to his mind the actual boy neither copied lawyers' briefs, nor handled an anvil, nor moulded iron. For in that world which he had created for himself he did nothing the livelong day but think and write poetry. Sometimes the poetry would be scribbled down in the short noon recess, but oftener the hours of the night were given to writing, rewriting, correcting, and revising the verse which he was sure must lead into the pleasant ways of life at last.

Whatever odd moments he had that were not given to writing poetry were spent in reading it. Out of his small salary his mother allowed him a little spending money, and with this he bought books. Usually they were second - hand volumes, picked up on street-stands, but occasionally a new book found its way to the library, which grew year by year, and was a mute record of the boy's ambitions. In this way Stoddard became familiar with the best English poetry, and so got an education not then to be had in many schools.

After several books of manuscript poetry had been filled and destroyed, for he seems to have understood that this writing was only a training, he at last ventured to offer a poem to a weekly magazine, which accepted it, and the young poet actually saw himself in print. About the same time he received some encouraging criticisms from the poet N. P. Willis, who saw a little volume of his manuscript. His most valuable acquaintance at this time was Mrs. Kirkland, the editor of a magazine, who not only praised the young poet, but bought some of his work for her magazine. Other successes followed, and finally Stoddard had saved enough money to have a volume of his poems published; although he only sold one copy of these poems, which was published under the title *Footprints*, it yet tended to help him materially, for it brought him to the notice of literary people. Like many another poet, Stoddard owed much of his success to the kindly and generous sympathy of older and successful writers. This little volume led to his being introduced to the best literary society of New York, and that was of inestimable value to the then unknown poet. In 1852, being then in his twenty-eighth year, Stoddard published a second volume of poems, and a year later, through the influence of Hawthorne, he obtained a position as clerk in the Custom House, a place which brought him an assured income, and yet gave leisure for his literary work.

In this same year he published two dainty volumes for children, *Fairy Land* and *Town and Country*. They are full of delightful humor and show the poet in one of his happiest moods.

The life of Stoddard has been emphatically that of the poet and student. His whole career has been colored by one ambition, the highest that can govern any writer, to succeed in his chosen calling and do honor to American literature. Besides his poems, which have passed through many editions since the appearance of his first little volume, he has been connected with various newspapers and has been the editor of a magazine. Among other things he has also edited *Griswold's Poets of America, The Female Poets of America*, an edition of the *Late English Poets*, and a collection of reminiscences of well-known writers known as the Bric-a-Brac Series. Since 1880 he has been editor of the literary department of the New York *Mail and Express*.

To all this miscellaneous work Stoddard has brought the trained intellect and artistic perception of the poet and student, and he has stamped much of it with more than an ephemeral value. His work on the *Mail and Express* is a weekly review of the literary work of the world, and is a good summary of the intellectual field of the day.

Some of the finest examples of his poems

are found in the collections, *Songs of Summer*, *The King's Bell* and *The Book of the East*. Single examples, such as the *Vanished May*, *Up in the Trees*, *The Grape Gatherer*, *Dead Leaves*, show his sense of beauty, mingled with the old Greek love of the earth, in perfect poetic union. In these moods he is a true descendant of the early poet worshippers of nature. *Wratislaw*, the story of a little hero prince, whose brave spirit wrought noble deeds in the days when the Turk overran Europe, is a beautiful specimen of the poet's art in dealing with legendary subjects. So also is his *Masque of the Three Kings*, in which the old Bible Christmas Story is told anew. A *Wedding Under the Directory* is a quaint picture of a day, relived by another generation. In 1876 Stoddard was asked for a poem to celebrate the opening of the Centennial Exposition, and responded with his *Guests of the State*, a noble composition, full of that large sympathy, which made the occasion a memorable one in the history of the nation.

The fact that most impresses one in regard to his work is his intense feeling for beauty. And in this sense one can trace his literary career from his earliest years. Such a nature must have unconsciously been nurtured in those exalted moods which are revealed only to the poet born. Through all his best work there is an undertone which is felt rather than seen, and which hints of a deeper current underneath.

Some of his most charming work appears in transcriptions of the poetry of the East—love-songs of the Tartar and Arab, of the Persian and the Sclav. With true poetic sympathy he has wrought these pictures of Eastern life into English verse that reveals all their own wild force and fire.

Stoddard's life has been spent almost entirely in New York. As he has devoted all his talent to his chosen work, so he has reaped the reward that comes from such high endeavor, and won in its best sense the poet's fame.

CHAPTER III

EDWARD EGGLESTON

1837—

In all the stories which relate to the settlement of the United States none are more interesting than those which tell of the experiences of the pioneers who fought face to face with the Indians in the valley of the Ohio.

From the time when Daniel Boone and his companions followed Indian trails across the Alleghenies and settled Kentucky, until far beyond the period of the Revolution, the history of every settlement on the frontier was one of bitter warfare with the red men. Before he could build his house or prepare the land for tilling, the frontiersman had to erect a blockhouse to protect the settlement against his wily foe, and very often this fort-like structure was the home for weeks at a time of the entire community. Whether the pioneer felled trees, broke up the new ground, sowed, tilled, or gathered his crops he worked ever with his rifle by his side. And the housewife, busy with spinning, weaving, and other family cares, never went to her door without an anxious glance to see that no lurking enemy was near. Very often, too, in spite of all precaution, the smoke rising from his burning dwelling would be the first warning that the settler would receive, and he would hasten home to find his wife and children slaughtered or carried away into captivity.

It required brave hearts to found homes on the frontier, where even nature gave only in return for hardest toil, and still braver ones to work steadily on in the face of treacherous Indian foes. But the pioneer of the Ohio Valley did not know fear, and his record of honorable accomplishment has made him a famous character in the story of his country.

An old block-house of this region, the first that was erected on the Indiana side of the Ohio, was built by Captain Craig, a noted pioneer, who won renown both as a fighter against the Indians and as a leader in the little band of settlers. It was men of this class, resolute, brave, and self-sacrificing, which redeemed the Valley of the Ohio from nature and the red man and made it habitable.

And although the struggle went on for years, it ended at last in peace and prosperity for the pioneers. The Indians retreated toward the Mississippi, thriving little villages grew up around the old block - houses, and the outlying country, rich in valuable timber or meadow lands, was as free from danger as the valleys of the Connecticut or Hudson.

In Vevay, Ind., one of these little villages, about four miles from the old block-house, was born on December 10, 1837, Edward Eggleston, a grandson of Captain Craig. His father, a descendant of a Virginia family which had won honor in the Revolution, was a prominent lawyer of Vevay, where the boy lived until his third year. The family then removed to the old Craig homestead, and in this region, so rich in historic memories, young

Eggleston spent six of the most impression-able years of his life. As he was a delicate boy, school life occupied a very small part of his time, though books were always interesting to him. He above all implored to be taught to write, and almost as soon as he knew how to write he began to express his own thoughts, of which he had many. But the best education he could have had for the work he was to do was obtained from the still lingering pictur-esqueness of Western life, which surrounded him everywhere.

Life was still primitive enough in the Ohio Valley, and the interests of the people were so closely allied that they seemed almost like one large family. If a man wished to build a house or barn, he summoned his neighbors to what was called "a raising," when all worked to raise the building on its foundations. The crop of corn was husked at a "bee," to which all the country lads and lasses came, and after dividing into two companies, worked hard till one or the other won the race by husking the last ear first. A supper in the farm-house kitchen and a dance in the barn would follow, when the guests would separate, to meet perhaps the next night at another "bee." Wood was chopped, logs rolled from the forests to the river, where they were floated down to the sawmills, and every other kind of farm work done in the same way. In the households the women had spinning and quilting "bees," and, in fact, from the oldest to the youngest, each member of the community felt that he had its interests at heart.

While the frontier life had developed a certain class who were rough in manner and careless in morals, the greater part of the people were Methodists, and were sincerely and enthusiastically devoted to their religion. In those widely scattered communities churches were almost unknown, and services were held in the school-rooms or at private houses, as might be most desirable. The ministers were as a rule men of character and force, descendants in the next generation of stalwart Indian fighters and frontiersmen, and into their work they put the same energy which their fathers and grandfathers had used in winning homes in the wilderness.

These Methodist ministers were called circuit-riders; they had no settled parish, but each one had charge of from fifty to one hundred parishes, which they were required to visit as often as possible. With his saddle-bags and rifle the circuit-rider would travel from village to village, claiming hospitality from the families under his care, who always welcomed him gladly, placed their houses at his disposal, and if the meeting was to be held in the school-house, stood ready to guard him from the attacks of any of the rough class who might try to interfere with him. The circuit-rider was undoubtedly the greatest influence for good known to the Ohio Valley, and his respect and esteem were sought by all. He did his work well, infusing into the daily life of his followers an earnest desire for right-doing and a hunger for spirituality which had a lasting effect upon the characters of the builders of the Middle West. One of Eggleston's first memories must have been that of the circuit-rider riding

3

up to the door of his grandfather's house and dismounting, while the heads of the family stood ready to welcome him with respectful courtesy. And the mind-picture photographed thus vividly was to be reproduced later and form a unique contribution to American literature.

From the old homestead the family removed to Vevay on the death of Eggleston's father, and here in his tenth year the boy began his school life in the little school-house which has become so familiar to his readers. The scenes and incidents of this experience are retold in that charming volume, *A Hoosier School Boy*, with so loving and faithful a touch that no one can doubt that they are the personal memories of the chronicler. The ambitions of these boys, whose greatest desire was to have an education, their hopes and disappointments, their misunderstandings with their teacher, and their manly apologies, their schoolboy games and plays, are all a part of Eggleston's own experience. The school-house is a memory, not a creation, and into it really walked one day the veritable little Christopher Columbus, with his tiny voice and thin legs, to shame all the big boys by reading better than they. Little Christopher Columbus did not know that his biographer sat watching him with admiring eyes, and no one dreamed that this episode was afterward to be incorporated into that charming book. Eggleston's boyhood, like that of Howells, was full of the energetic influence of the young West, an influence which, after building homes in the wilderness and bringing civilization to take the place of savage conditions, kept bravely to its work of developing the frontier.

The youth of that period received only those things for which he strived. Education, the boon more desired than anything else, was hard to obtain. The country schools were either taught by old fogies, who ruled with birch and rattan, or by young men, to whom teaching meant only a means to livelihood while preparing for some other work. Here and there throughout the country were scattered a few academies where the higher branches were taught, but only a few boys had the means to avail themselves of the privilege. The boy of the Ohio Valley fifty years ago knew very early that his own will and strength must win for him in the battle of life; and this knowledge brought into play the best forces of his nature. Underneath the carelessness of boyhood generally lurked an earnest desire to become useful to his generation, and to this ambition Eggleston was no exception.

Life meant much to him early, and at nine years old the village school at Vevay knew no better pupil than the delicate boy who had already begun to learn that the patient endurance of ill-health must be one of his greatest teachers. A few weeks at school would be followed by many months of sickness, but his purpose never faltered. During one of these periods of ill-health he was sent to stay for some months in a backwoods district, where life was still in the rudest stage. Shut off from books, Eggleston gathered from this experience stores of valuable knowledge. Although only twelve years old, he was a student of human nature, and the unfamiliar scenes became picture-stories of the lives of the rough men by whom he was surrounded. Many years after he reproduced the memories of these days with a faithfulness which showed how vividly they had impressed him. There is, indeed, in all his work the same charm that is found in the poetry of Whittier, and which makes so much of it seem like a translation of the moods and feelings of boyhood.

Besides studying, Eggleston was always busy writing. He was still a young boy when his first contribution appeared. A country newspaper had offered a prize for the best composition by a schoolboy under fifteen, and he resolved to obtain it if possible. He was not at that time in school, but was acting as clerk for a hardware merchant. The editor, however, assured him that this would not debar him from the competition. Thereafter every spare moment was given to the composition of an essay on the given subject, and to Eggleston's great joy he won the prize, although his em-

ployer had from that day suspicions as to the
real value of a clerk with a literary turn of
mind.

Not very long after, being again at school,
he won high praise from his teacher for a little essay on *The Will*, which, although full of
imitations of the writers he had been studying,
still showed much promise. At that time there
were no railroads connecting the East and
the West, and the newspapers and books from
the Atlantic coast were a long time in reaching the frontier. There grew up, therefore,
in the Ohio Valley a little coterie of native
writers, who represented the best thought and
culture of the region. Their poetry, fiction,
and essays were gladly welcomed by the Western newspapers, which often devoted pages to
this literature, and the writers thus gained
much local fame. The teacher who so kindly
encouraged young Eggleston was one of the
best known of these Western writers. Although she found fault with every other sen-
tence of the little essay on *The Will*, she still
saw its merits, and to Eggleston, who had ad-

mired her fame for years, her praise was very sweet. It was a great inspiration to him at the moment, and the faithful criticism which she continued to give was of inestimable value to the future novelist.

When he was seventeen Eggleston went to Virginia to visit his father's relatives. Here he had a year's experience of Southern plantation life. This easy, luxurious existence was a great contrast to life in the Ohio Valley, but, although Eggleston appreciated it, his instincts remained true to the wider freedom of the country of his birth. He was destined to be the chronicler of the true story of much of that Western life, and nothing could ever detract from its vital and enduring charm. One of his Virginia uncles, who was rich and childless, wished to adopt him, but Eggleston refused, and returned home richer for the experience and for the few months' training from an excellent Virginia school, but still devoted heart and soul to the interests of the West.

A year later he was sent to Minnesota, in the

hope that the climate might benefit his health, which seemed completely broken. He was threatened with consumption, and knowing that he had but this chance for life, he threw himself desperately into the rough frontier work, which kept him out of doors continually. He drove oxen to break up new ground, wading through the wet prairie grass at daybreak, and broiling under the noonday sun. He felled trees, rolled logs, and acted as chain-bearer for a party of surveyors. He fought a troublesome cough and fever with the same determination, and in a few months his youth and pluck had turned the scale, and he was on the road to health. He now set out to walk from Minnesota to Kansas, and it is a pity that he kept no journal of this experience.

A delicate boy travelling through the Western frontier for over two hundred miles, he must have met with many unique adventures. He slept at night in hunters' cabins, rough country taverns, little log-houses of settlers, and sometimes out of doors under the shelter of friendly logs and ties. He lived on the rude fare that supplied the wants of the hardy backwoodsmen, and his companions were oftenest those rough spirits who found in the excitement of frontier life a congenial atmosphere. But the journey was accomplished, though on reaching Kansas he was not allowed to enter its borders because of the unsettled state that society had been thrown into by the political troubles. Turning eastward, Eggleston resolved to travel home on foot. When near the end of his journey his money and strength both nearly gave out, and he was indebted to two friendly strangers for the two dollars necessary to reach home. He arrived at the house of his nearest relatives in such a tattered condition that the maid almost refused him entrance, and his half-brother was for some moments in doubt about allowing the relationship. This experience ended Eggleston's boyhood. The next year, being not yet nineteen, he put into execution a long-cherished plan. Knowing that his health would never allow him to enter college, he put that

wish aside, and filled with a desire to make
of life a noble achievement, he became that
ideal of the young West, a circuit-rider.

In entering the ministry Eggleston was ful-
filling the hope of his life. To one of his education and training the Methodist minister
of the day represented the ideal of self-sacrifice and spiritual aspiration; he was a soldier
of Christ, ready to fight, conquer or die, in
his Master's service, and to him the warfare
seemed glorious. Eggleston took up his new
duties as the youth of old assumed the honors
of knighthood. It was a solemn dedication of
his young life to the service of humanity and
the acceptance of a trust which he faithfully fulfilled. The Methodism inherited and
shared by the generations to which Eggleston
belonged did for the West what Puritanism
accomplished for New England—it made the
every-day life an impulse toward right-doing,
and in this it laid strong and deep the foundations of noble character and loyal citizenship.
The republic owes much to this valiant army
of workers which Eggleston now joined, burn-

ing with a desire to devote his whole feeble strength to the common cause.

We can picture him thus, a delicate boy, riding from place to place, be the weather what it might, finding his home among the members of his scattered flock, suffering discomfort and often danger, anxious, yet fearing nothing but that he might fail in his duty.

His first charge included a circuit of ten places, which he visited at intervals. He carried his wardrobe in his saddle-bags, and as he never for one moment gave up his determination to become a scholar, nearly all the time he spent on horseback was passed in reading and study.

Much of Eggleston's experience as an itinerant Methodist minister is reproduced in *The Circuit Rider*. The Ohio Valley in Eggleston's youth was the border-land of town and village life, all the great country westward being occupied only by Indians or by rough settlements of hunters, traders, and miners. This place between, where the civilization of the East met the wild life of the West, was the scene of *The Circuit Rider*, into whose pages are wrought many striking incidents of those successful times. The heroes of the book are two youths, Kike and Morton, sons of valley farmers. Both are turned from their wild lives through the influence of one of those Methodist ministers so familiar to their times, and both renounce all worldly ambitions to enter upon the life of the circuit-rider. The story is touchingly in sympathy with the experience of the humble country folk who figure in its pages. Their home life and their spiritual struggles alike appeal to our interest; we are present at their merry corn-huskings and apple-paring bees, at their prayer-meetings, and camp-meetings. Each scene has the value of local history, and nowhere in American literature is there a more soul-stirring picture than that which traces Kike awakening to the high conception of a life of self-sacrifice.

Eggleston's own experience as a circuit-rider came to an end after six months, as his health broke down completely under the strain, and he was obliged to return to Minnesota. The invigorating air and freedom from care again worked their charm, and in a short time he was once more engaged in preaching. His work now was on the Minnesota frontier, where the Indians still lingered, forming a large part of the population. The white settlements and Indian villages all along the Minnesota River soon became familiar with the face of the young preacher, who walked from place to place shod in moccasins, and who brought into their rough lives the only refining and uplifting influence that they knew. We can see the groups gathered round him while he gives his word of advice or encouragement, the scene recalling an episode in the career of Eliot, and reflecting a phase of American life that has forever passed away.

But Eggleston's fame as a preacher soon made him in demand in the larger towns, and less than two years after he entered the ministry he accepted a call to the city of St. Paul. From this time his life was spent almost entirely in cities. Owing to his poor health he was often obliged to give up his duties as a minister and take up whatever work presented itself as a means of support for his family. He had in the meantime begun to write regularly for various religious papers, and had successfully accomplished some editorial work.

In 1870, when Eggleston was in his thirty-fourth year, he accepted a position on *The Independent*, and left the West for his new home in Brooklyn. Although later years were again devoted to preaching, this was the beginning of an uninterrupted literary life, which has continued to the present day.

His first important book, and the one which brought him instant recognition, was *The Hoosier Schoolmaster*, which was written as a serial for the periodical *Hearth and Home*. Almost immediately after its publication in book form it was issued in England, France, Germany, and Denmark, and everywhere it was received with the greatest favor. With true artistic instinct, Eggleston had gone for the material of his book to the old familiar life of his youth. The scenes which lingered in his memory when touched by his trained hand became vivid pictures of new and peculiar interest. This revelation of the picturesqueness of Western frontier life appealed to all, and the vital humanity which throbbed through its pages touched every heart.

This book which made Eggleston a novelist showed him, also, the probable place for his own contributions to American literature. He became the novelist of the river frontier and prairie life, which so fortunately for our literature lingered long enough to make its lasting impression upon his youth. The titles of his successive books show this life in many aspects. From the ideal reproductions of *The Hoosier Schoolmaster*, and *The Hoosier Schoolboy*, in which we walk hand in hand with childhood, through all the graver problems of adult life we still follow the fortunes of the class that Eggleston's art has made typical.

One of the most interesting of his books is *The Graysons*, the story of a young law-student who is accused of murder, and whose acquittal is obtained by Abraham Lincoln who pleads his cause. This introduction of Lincoln into fiction was made by request, and the incident is cleverly made to illustrate the keenness and sagacity of the great statesman even while an obscure lawyer in an obscurer Western town.

Among Eggleston's juvenile works *The Schoolmaster's Stories for Boys and Girls*, *Queer Stories for Boys and Girls*, *A First Book in American History*, and a large amount of miscellaneous matter all indicate his sympathy with the heart of childhood, and his ability to enter into the questions and interests which make up the child-world. They are genuine boys and girls who walk through his pages. Perhaps the book which shows Eggleston at his best is *The Circuit Rider*, with its fine insight into those spiritual problems which interest all humanity. *Roxy* is another delineation of character, which, in its story of the struggle between right and wrong in the human heart, suggests the old Puritanism of New England.

Besides his novels Eggleston has accomplished a great deal of work on historical subjects, which has appeared in various magazines and periodicals, and he has in preparation a history of the United States to which he has already devoted much time in research in the great libraries of the world. Some school histories and a good portion of miscellaneous matter must also be included in his work. His distinctive contribution to American literature is his reproduction of a phase of American life which has now passed away, but which has a unique value for the student of history.

The latter years of Eggleston's life have been spent mostly in New York, where he now lives.

4

CHAPTER IV

CHARLES DUDLEY WARNER

1829 —

Charles Dudley Warner was born in Plain-
field, Mass., in that lovely and picturesque region which has become celebrated in American literature as the birthplace of William Cul-
len Bryant. The country has scarcely changed
since those early days when the boy Bryant
used to wander over its fields and hills and
hear in the neighboring forests the cries of the
wolves and bears which made their home there.
The Warner family belonged to the farmer
race, which at that time made up the larger
part of New England life. The father was a
man of fine tastes, having a good library and
being in frequent correspondence with people
in various parts of the country who were interested in the public questions of the day.

But while Charles was still a very young child
his father died, and the family was broken up
for some years. The boy was taken to the
home of an aunt, who owned a homestead on
the Deerfield River, and it is here that his first
recollections centre. The lad's first school was
in one of those little school-houses which have
been described in the verses of Whittier and
Bryant, and his life may in every respect be
said to have corresponded to that so lovingly
portrayed in "The Barefoot Boy." This life
makes a boy healthful and manly, and the close
communion with nature fosters those poetic
impressions to which the young mind is so sus-
ceptible. Warner was happy in the care of his
aunt and an older cousin, but there was one
great drawback to this otherwise contented
life. At the Deerfield farm-house there were
no books except the Bible and one or two religious works, and to a book-loving boy this
was a great deprivation. The family held to
the strict observance of the New England Sab-
bath, which extended from six o'clock on Saturday evening to six o'clock on Sunday even-

ing, and though much of this time was occupied with church-going, there were many hours
in which a book would have been a boon.
The imaginative child, however, has always a
little kingdom of his own to which he may retreat when disappointed with the actual world,
and in this fairy realm Warner spent many
a happy hour planning and dreaming of the
future. He was but repeating the experience
of so many other New England boys in whose
early days seems to have lain the best training
for the intellectual life.

But a lack of reading does not make a boy
poor when he has at command the fruits of
meadow, field, and wood; when trout-streams
exist for him alone; when sunny days and rainy
weather alike have their special joys, and when
nature is forever watching a chance to teach
him lessons of truth and beauty. The atmosphere of this quiet, uneventful life was an influence for good—an influence which Warner
afterward gratefully appreciated.

Many a boy whose actual life has been
bounded by the narrow confines of farm life

has had his first glimpse of the world beyond
through the pages of a book. In Warner's
case this book was the *Arabian Nights,* which
his seat-mate brought to the little school-house
one day and hid amid the other boyish treasures in his desk. A district school-teacher cannot see all that happens in his restless kingdom, and the urchin had more than one stolen
glance into the wonderful book while he was
supposed to be studying his spelling or doing
sums. And what an ideal world this was
which the young discoverer had thus sailed
into! Here were genii, fairies, enchanted car-
pets, valleys of diamonds, and masquerading
pedlers who gave "old lamps for new." In
this realm, which the geographies so ignorantly
omitted to mention, farm work and even farm
pleasures had no place. All was glittering,
dazzling, beautiful! Every day held new adventures, and one's intimate friends owned
miles of treasure - houses and inexhaustible
mines of wealth. When school was done Warner succeeded in borrowing this treasure, and
hurrying home, announced to his aunt and

cousin that he had found "the most splendid book in the world." Imagine his surprise and disgust when these relatives, after an inspection of the precious volume, said, gravely: "No, you cannot read this, Charles, it is not true."

But the boy evidently thinking that in such cases aunts and cousins were as fallible as primary geographies, carried the book to the barn and hid it in the hay, and there spent many an hour devouring the enchanting tales.

Another book which he began at this time was *Cook's Voyages Around the World*, the second volume of which had drifted somehow up to the old farm-house door. These two books with the Bible were absolutely all that Warner knew of the vast treasures of literature while he remained at the Deerfield River farm.

But life broadened into wider channels when in his twelfth year he was taken by his mother to Cazenovia, N. Y., and placed in the academy there. The life at Deerfield had been that of the river, and fields, and woods, but at Cazenovia Warner became emphatically the studious boy, to whom books and study meant

more than anything else in the world. At the
academy he was fortunate in his boy ac-
quaintances, and there he made friendships
which have lasted through his life. One of
his friends was the son of a bookseller, in
whose shop Warner was allowed to browse at
will. And here he learned to know Irving
and Cooper, Hawthorne, Prescott, and Bryant, and the other writers who were founding American literature. This education
which went on outside the academy was also
greatly stimulated by the talks and discussions
on literary matters between him and his comrades. And by and by, as always happens in
the case of boys who read and read, they all
began to write. Their first efforts took the
form of poetry, which somehow always seems
to the boyish mind the easiest thing to write,
and thenceforth much of their interest in life
lay in listening to and criticising one another's
verses. One of these boys while still a youth
wrote that celebrated song of how

> In their ragged regimentals
> The old Continentals

rallied to the defence of American liberty in the stormy days of the Revolution.

Another has since become a famous scholar in literature and the arts, whose name is known to two continents. Warner himself, who soon forsook poetry for prose, can date his literary career from these days when his chief ambition was to write and to write well. It was his habit then and long afterward to walk up and down his room while writing and repeat the sentences over and over, changing and polishing them until they sounded rhythmic. The study of the best poetry of America and England still went on steadily, and the boys often played a guessing game as to author and verse. Sometimes the giver of the verse would slip in a couplet of his own, and then laugh at the wild guesses which placed his effusions among the English classics.

One of the most luminous memories of Warner's youth is that of a visit to Irving at Sunnyside, whither he went under the guidance of one of these early friends. The famous author received his young admirers kindly and gave to Warner an ivy-leaf from the vine which had grown from a slip plucked from the cottage of Burns's " Bonnie Jean." Neither giver nor receiver foresaw, then, the link that was to be established later by Warner's biography of America's first great man of letters.

In 1851 Warner was graduated from Hamilton College, which he entered from Cazenovia Academy, taking the first prize for English. He had already become somewhat known to the literary world through contributions to the *Knickerbocker* and *Putnam's Magazine* and from occasional visits to New York, when he became for a time a member of that Bohemian world in which the younger generation of writers lived.

But although he had made a good beginning, literature was exchanged two years after his graduation for the wild life of the Mexican frontier, whither he went with a surveying party in 1853. After this experience he studied law and practised it in Chicago for a few years. But in 1866 he returned to his first ambition, and became editor of the *Hartford*

Press, which a year later was incorporated with the *Courant*. Warner made of this newspaper one of the best-edited journals of its class, and in its conduct won an enviable reputation as an editor.

A year or two later he took his first journey to Europe, and on his return contributed those papers to the *Courant* which in 1870 made their appearance in book-form under the title *My Summer in a Garden*. It is in this little volume that Warner struck that vein of humor which makes his work a delight to his large audience.

Another book which added greatly to his reputation at this time is that called *Saunterings*, which contains his impressions of Europe in this first journey. Very much of Warner's work has for its background his journeyings in Europe and at home. His *Winter on the Nile, In the Levant*, and *Notes of a Roundabout Journey in Europe* are among his most delightful reminiscences of foreign travel, while *Studies in the South, Studies in the Great West*, and *Our Italy*, show his wide

familiarity with the scenes of his native land.
He is a sympathetic, cultivated traveller, by
whom new impressions of art and social life
are appreciated, but who, nevertheless, sees all
things through that half-humorous light which
delights American readers. He is never too
learned to extract fun out of a pyramid or cliff
dwelling, and, though an ardent patriot, he has
no hesitation in laughing at the foibles and
eccentricities of his countrymen. His charac-
terizations of foreign and home life possess all
the flavor and freshness of the mind which
looks at life from a new point of view. He is
the author of some charming essays, printed
as *Back Log Studies* and *As We Were Saying*,
and he has published several successful novels.
If he is not a creator in the realm of art, he is
a keen observer and man of the world, deeply
interested in his fellow-travellers. His records
of his impressions, although thrown into the
form of novels, are valuable chiefly for their
sympathetic view of every-day life.

One of our author's most charming books
is that reminiscence of his childhood, *Being a*

Boy. Here we have the actual life of the New England boy sixty years ago. All the little humble incidents of farm life, all the simple pleasures, the delights of fishing and nutting, of maple-sugar gathering, and the first party are noted with a sincerity that makes the little narrative genuine history. Whittier read this book more than once, and said it was a page out of his own life-story. Outside its literary merit it is valuable as one more truthful picture of the simple life of New England; a life whose healthful duties and pleasures left wide spaces for the soul to grow up to noble conceptions of manhood.

Besides his other work Mr. Warner has contributed a department to *Harper's Magazine*, and has made some valuable additions to the social science papers of the day. He has also served on the commission for establishing prison reform, and he is well known as a successful lecturer. Throughout his career he has followed mainly the lines laid down for himself in his student days, and has bounded his ambitions by the literary life. Since 1867 his home has been at Hartford. One of our most successful humorists, he is also a striking example of those earnest toilers whose work well supports the dignity of American literature.

CHAPTER V

EDMUND CLARENCE STEDMAN

1833—

Out of the many New England country boys who dreamed day-dreams one came back in manhood to his early home and confessed that some of his dreams had come true. This was not strange, for it is generally the youthful day-dreamer whose after-life is fullest of accomplishment. Nature, who is so wise a teacher, sends in these dreams such a vision of the future that the soul is even then eager to press forward to its realization. Sometimes this vision is obscured later by ambitions that are ignoble; in such cases it fades away and is lost, like youth itself. But the larger number of those who do the world's noblest work is made up of men and women who received in childhood some such revelation of the meaning of life. If with the day-dream comes a sense of the beauty of nature—of the melodies which thrill through the songs of brook, and bird, and forest aisle—and a desire to reproduce them, the boy is apt to become a poet. Such a boy was Edmund Clarence Stedman, born at Hartford, Ct., in 1833, being the son of a merchant in comfortable circumstances.

When he was two years old Stedman was taken to Norwich to live with a great-uncle, and it was with this pretty village, with its elm-shaded streets and old colonial mansions, and with its outlying fields and pasture lands, that his earliest associations are connected. In his poem, *The Freshet*, there are many touches which recall his boyhood, and which are in a sense biographical. The pictures of the group of boys standing on the bridge or wading through the alder thickets to the deep channel, where they fished and swam, and of the spring freshet when the river rolled on like a flood, carrying cakes of ice, lumber, rails, hay, and cattle along, are both scenes from the actual experiences of the poet's youth. Throughout all his work one hears, indeed, an ever-recurrent note that tells of early days ; sometimes the note is sad and sometimes gay, but always it is touched with that regret which clings to the past.

The uncle with whom Stedman passed his youth was an eminent lawyer and a man of learning. Very careful attention was paid to the boy's education, as well as to the home life, which was carried on after the strictest New England fashion. But Stedman, like other New England boys, was all the better for this discipline. It developed strength and endurance of character, a manliness of temper, and an indifference to the minor ills of life, and this is invaluable training for any poet. Stedman entered Yale at sixteen, and immediately became known as one of its cleverest freshmen, though he rebelled often at the discipline. He was a brilliant member of the college literary circle and a contributor to the *Yale Literary Magazine*, which bestowed a prize upon him for a poem on Westminster Abbey.

But his record as a scholar did not blind the college authorities to his faults, and in his junior year the faculty suspended him for some boyish escapade, and he never returned. Twenty years afterward, however, when Yale had reason to be proud of his fame as a man of letters, she called him to her halls and conferred upon him his degree in the presence of an assemblage called together to see him thus honored both as man and poet.

The immediate result of his leaving college was a determination to begin life for himself, and at the age of nineteen he became editor of the *Norwich Tribune*. The new venture was at once successful. Two years later he took charge of the *Winsted Herald*, and conducted it so successfully that it speedily acquired the fame of being one of the cleverest newspapers published outside the great cities. But gratifying as this must have been, the young editor sighed for new fields, and in 1852 he removed to New York and became a contributor to *Harper's* and *Putnam's Magazines*, and a short-lived periodical published under the name of *Vanity Fair*. Stedman was now twenty-one years old. He had married, and as his

5

magazine work could not support him, he returned to journalism. His first important literary success, as in the case of Lowell and Holmes, was based upon the publication of a political poem.

The newspapers had just given to the world the story of John Brown's capture of Harper's Ferry, and North and South alike were bitterly excited over the event. This plain farmer was the most humble of the anti-slavery leaders, yet his name was destined to be the war-cry of the North for four years. He had, with a force of men, marched to the fortress of Harper's Ferry with the avowed purpose of starting a military crusade against slavery. The garrison, under the impression that a large force was attacking, surrendered without a struggle, and John Brown marched in and took possession. The fort was retaken in a few days, but the event produced the most extraordinary agitation all over the country. Every newspaper published an account of it, and it was feared that the most serious results would follow.

What should be done with John Brown himself became a burning question, the South clamoring for his death and the North demanding his acquittal. While his fate was still under discussion there appeared in the *New York Tribune* a remarkable poem, in which all the feeling of the moment seemed crystallized. Stedman was the author of this poem, and no one but a true poet could so have entered into the spirit of the old hero, to whom inaction seemed a denial of principle.

"How John Brown Took Harper's Ferry" is a ballad full of fire and force. Stedman's power is shown in his fine appreciation of the unselfish frenzy which possessed the old man and led him to offer himself as a martyr in the cause he had espoused. One of the most stirring ballads produced by the war, it will always hold a prominent place in the lyric poetry of America. In less than two years after its publication the author found himself war correspondent of the *Tribune*, following the fortunes of the Army of the Potomac in its first campaign. The South had decided that the question of slavery must be settled by the sword, and the country was in the midst of civil war.

Another poem published in the *Tribune* about the time of the John Brown episode showed the versatile talent of the new poet. This was "The Diamond Wedding," a satire on the marriage of a young society girl to a wealthy Cuban planter. A list of his gifts to his promised bride appeared in the daily papers, and sounded like a catalogue of the treasures of Haroun-al-Rashid. Stedman's poem struck the popular fancy, which was also pleased by the publication of a song on the charms of " Lager Bier." Encouraged by this friendly eulogy, he published a volume of poems under the title *Poems Lyric and Idyllic*. It is in this volume that "The Freshet" occurs, and also, among several other good examples, the poem "Penelope," in which the old Greek legend is retold in beautiful verse, which not only showed Stedman's mastery of blank verse, but also his fine scholarship.

Stedman followed the fortunes of the army

throughout the war, his letters to his journal forming a valuable contribution to the war literature of the day. He saw the first famous Battle of Bull Run, when the Northern army was forced to retreat, and when it seemed for the time that the war would be carried into the North. A reminiscence of his experience in camp and hospital, on march and battle-field, is found in his long poem, "Alice of Monmouth." But, although this poem possesses passages of remarkable beauty, it does not show Stedman at his highest reach. This is attained in those shorter lyrics, which are so spontaneous, so full of natural poetry and so perfect in art that they seem to spring unconsciously from the soul. One cannot help regretting that our poet has not given us a more generous measure of them. One of the most perfect of these lyrics, "The Doorstep," is full of that tender regret which breathes through all the poet's work a treasured memory of happy youth. "Country Sleighing" is another song of nature, full of the dash and breezy story of the country winter season. Again in " Holyoke Valley" the poet still looks backward to his boyhood, and gives, through the music of poetry, one more bright picture of the past. Among his other poems may be mentioned the ode delivered before the graduating class of Dartmouth College in 1873, called "The Dartmouth Ode," and a beautiful and touching tribute to Horace Greeley, delivered at the request of the Printers' Association at the unveiling of the bust of Greeley in Greenwood Cemetery. Among other poems of occasions are the fine lines, "Gettysburg," delivered at the reunion of the Army of the Potomac in 1871, and a monody on the death of Bryant, delivered at the Century Club, New York.

Outside his poetry Stedman is known as a most conscientious and scholarly editor of the work of other writers and as a critic of original and thoughtful mind. He has edited, in conjunction with Thomas Bailey Aldrich, a choice selection of the works of Landor, and in 1875 he began the publication in *Scribner's Magazine* of a series of critical articles on the poets and poetry of the Victorian Age, which forms one of the most valuable works of criticism in our later literature. Following this came a volume of essays, called "The Poets of America," and one entitled "The Nature and Elements of Poetry"—a critical and imaginative study. He has edited also *The Library of American Literature*, and an anthology of Victorian poetry, and made a scholarly translation of the Greek idyllic poets. In all his literary productions Stedman shows not only his fine poetic gift, but the sound literary judgment and attainments of the scholar, and his work forms a valuable contribution to American letters.

Stedman has passed the greater part of his life in New York, whither he returned soon after the war, and where he has found opportunity not only to write books but to be a successful business man.

CHAPTER VI

BRET HARTE

1839—

One of the favorite stories told by the men who had conquered Mexico and Peru was that of a region of fabulous wealth, situated somewhere in the region of the Sierra Madre Mountains, and ruled by California, a white queen of divine origin. There, it was said, were hidden mines of unexhaustible treasures, where emeralds, diamonds, and rubies were as plentiful as gold and silver. There, also, the rain and dew watered the most beautiful valleys in the world; the climate was beneficent, and it was suspected that there would be found that magic fountain of life, for which the brave De Leon had sought in vain. Many bands of adventurers, bold of heart and full of hope, roamed the valleys and toiled through the mountain passes in search of this wealth, but their effort was unrewarded. The mountains kept their secret, and no glimpse of diamond mine or wondrous fountain or beautiful queen was ever revealed. At length the quest was given up. The Spaniards built homes around the missions established by the priests, and with the help of the Indians they tilled the soil, planted vineyards, and were content with the plentiful annual harvests. Gradually little villages grew up and the country became settled. But it remained Spanish, many of the inhabitants being descendants of those old adventurers who had first come hither in search of gold.

For three hundred years peace and content reigned in the valleys; then, in a moment, all things were changed, as if by magic, by the discovery of gold in the Sacramento Valley. California had, by the treaty with Mexico, which ended the Mexican War, become a part of the United States. The news of the great discovery had to be carried by sailing-vessel around Cape Horn to the East, but no sooner

was it received than there began a wild rush
for the Pacific coast. These adventurers were
not dressed in doublet and hose, like the Spanish cavaliers, nor did they sail in those gaily
decked vessels with which the old Greeks loved
to propitiate fortune. They came instead from
every class, and they travelled in any conceiv-
able conveyance that could be placed on wheels;
many, indeed, went on foot, for the voyage was
long and expensive, and the overland route
was in the main preferred. Every country in
Europe sent emigrants to swell the numbers of
the gold-seekers, and soon the prairies and
plains of the West seemed alive with the wagon
trains, which kept close together from fear of
the Indians.

When the gold-fields were at last reached
they were soon taken possession of by the adventurers, who had turned soldiers in a common cause. Their camp-fires gleamed from
valley, and hill, and mountain pass, and the entire country was turned into a great camp.

Many of the towns of California had been
deserted in the first rush, and as the trades-

people, farmers, and mechanics were equally
engaged in the search for gold, all other business was for the time being paralyzed. It became almost impossible to buy the ordinary
articles of food and clothing, and any chance
vessel which was willing to dispose of its cargo
might do so at fabulous prices.

Wigwams, tents, brush-huts, and log-houses
served as dwellings for Americans, Mexicans,
Germans, Frenchmen, Austrians, Hollanders,
Chinese, and men of other nationalities, who
lived and worked side by side, shared one another's hopes and disappointments and successes, and made it apparent that in the miners'
camp at least all men were brothers.

During the early years of the California emigration, when the first excitement had abated,
but while all the picturesque elements of the
life still remained, there came to the gold-fields
a bright boy, who had left his home in Albany,
N. Y., to better his fortunes in the West. This
was Francis Bret Harte, whose father had been
a teacher in an Albany seminary. The boy
himself tried teaching on his arrival, but the

attempt was unsuccessful, and he turned his attention to mining. And here, because he was a poet, he saw many things that escaped the eyes of others. Here, where the cultivated man of Oxford or Harvard University worked with pick and pan beside the German peasant and unlettered Chinese, he saw a new picture of life, but still a true picture, because it reflected human nature. His finer sense grasped the poetry, the courage, and the heroism that often inspired this eager search for gold. He understood how the hope of the common laborer and the dream of the scholar might spring from unselfishness, and he saw that here, as on other fields, battles were lost nobly as well as nobly won. He saw, too, that as years went on all the foreign elements which made up the California of that day would blend to furnish a unique page of American history. And because it is the office of literature to record history, he believed that whoever should preserve in prose and verse the every-day scenes of that strange life would be doing valuable work.

His life at the mines was hardly more successful than had been his school-teaching experience, and by and by he became a compositor in a printing-office. Soon afterward he composed his first article in type without previously writing it down, and so his literary career began. A little later he entered the office of the *San Francisco Era*, then an important newspaper on the Pacific slope. While in this position he published anonymously a few sketches of life on the frontier. These stories, so full of the genuine flavor of the mining-camp, attracted some attention, but no one dreamed that they heralded a new voice in American literature. Ten years after the discovery of gold a magazine was organized in California under the title *The Overland Monthly*, and Bret Harte was made its editor. In the second issue of the magazine he published his story, "The Luck of Roaring Camp," which showed how rich was the material that lay in the life of the far West and revealed the impress of a master hand in literary composition. In California, however, the story was

not very popular. There the people who read
at all found their enjoyment in the books and
magazines familiar to cultivated society. Into
the miners' camps came copies of *The Edin-
burgh Review* and *Punch,* but the true meaning
of the life of which they themselves formed a
part had not yet been presented to these eager
adventurers.

But in the East "The Luck of Roaring
Camp" was received with enthusiastic praise.
The Atlantic Monthly at once offered to buy
similar sketches from the author — who had
not made himself known — and other periodicals and reviews spoke generous words in
favor of the young adventurer into this new
world of art. Bret Harte became famous almost in a day, and henceforth it was his task
to fulfil his boyish dream and put into literary
form those records of an experience that was
rapidly passing away. Sketches, stories, poems,
and novels followed closely upon one another.
He left no phase of this many-sided life untouched, and the series grew at last into a
faithful record of the most picturesque and

romantic episode of American history. What
diverse characters came to the writer's side and
claimed his attention as he wrote! Sometimes
it was a miner who had failed in his quest;
sometimes a Mexican *ranchero* with his light
heart and merry love-song; sometimes a con-
vict who had escaped from prison and was
trying life anew in the freedom of the camps.
Often it would be a little child who would seem
to tell its story to this ever-listening ear,—a
waif, perhaps, who had drifted into that wild
company, which yet kept its reverence for the
innocence of childhood. More than once the
hero of the occasion would be one of those
wild beasts who found their homes in the vast-
nesses of the mountain forests, a grizzly, watching with a dignified sense of his power the
incomprehensible antics of man, or a coyote
slinking along a dusty road. For each and
all the author became a faithful chronicler, and
because he had the true poet's insight he became more than a mere chronicler. He lifted
all this motley assemblage forever out of the
common-place of their rough lives and showed

that each was still real man or woman and
genuine kin to his race. Only a great artist
could have done this. Only genius could have
so looked beneath the exterior and found there
the living signs of the brotherhood of man;
the same genius which saw but a humbler
brother still in the ugly shape of Bruin, and
to whom the lazy coyote became only a "beg-
ging friar" living righteously upon the largess
of others.

As a background to his stories Bret Harte
paints in scenes of extraordinary natural beauty. He shows us, under the sunlight or
wrapped in storms, still set in their own atmosphere of loneliness, the rude camps and settlements, the rivers and cañons, which are the
haunts of his characters. The writer is, indeed, the poet of nature as well as of the heart,
and can reach easily her varying moods.

Among the most interesting of the stories
which relate to child-life are "A Waif of the
Plains," the story of two children who were
separated from their party during the overland
march to California; "The Christmas Gift that

Came to Rupert," the history of a drummer-boy; "Wan Lee," the life of a little Chinese boy in San Francisco; "The Story of Mliss," a miner's child, and "The Queen of the Pirate Island," a delightful conception, possible only to that land of bold adventure and tempting treasure. Perhaps it would not be out of the way to include among these juvenile chronicles the story of "A Boy's Dog" and the delightful experience of "Baby Sylvester," a fascinating bear cub, who was adopted by a young miner, and fed on the only milk that ever reached the settlement—for which service Adams' Express made special trips. He could play tag, roll down hill, take the cork out of the syrup-bottle with his teeth, dance, and shake hands, and when he arrived at maturity he was still faithful to his friends, and showed an ugly temper only to such human beings as annoyed him.

Bret Harte's poems, like his prose, preserve the varying conditions of early frontier life. They include also many verses written during the Civil War, among which "John Burns of Gettysburg," "Caldwell of Springfield," "The

6

Reveillé," and "How Are You, Sanitary?" are the most notable. Here, too, is found that exquisite little idyl, "Battle Bunny," the story of a white rabbit which was scared from its hiding-place and took refuge in a soldier's bosom as the two armies faced each other before battle.

Some of his best verses are written in the dialect of the camps, and are full of his own delightful, distinctive pathos and humor. "Jim," "Dow's Flat," "Plain Language from Truthful James," "Babes in the Wood," and "The Hawk's Nest" are among those that thus reproduce some characteristic incidents of the wild life. His poem, "The Heathen Chinee," was not intended for publication, but was written as a harmless skit for the amusement of two or three comrades. When a sudden exigency of the magazine dragged it from the reluctant author's portfolio, from Maine to California a delighted public laughed over it, but Mr. Harte himself has always lamented the fate that based so much of his literary reputation on a bit of unfair doggerel.

Although he has spent years abroad, both as United States Consul to different European cities and as a traveller, Bret Harte's work remains distinctly American. The collection of stories now numbers nearly thirty volumes; most of the titles, as *The Schoolmistress of Red Gulch, Snow-Bound at Eagles, Two Men of Sandy Bar*, and *Tennessee's Partner*, indicate the scene or nature of the sketch.

He is the historian of one of the most interesting movements in the progress of the United States—a movement which began while California was still a land of Mexican traditions, of grain and cattle-raising, and ended only when it took its place as one of the most important States of the Union. No one but an eye-witness could have written this history faithfully, and American literature owes one of its greatest debts to the man whose genius has thus illuminated the pages of the nation's life.

CHAPTER VII

1825-1878

When William Penn stood under the trees and made his famous treaty with the Indians there was in his company a young Quaker, whose descendants continued for generations to be honored citizens of Pennsylvania. As time went on the family mixed its Quaker blood with that of some neighboring German Lutherans. In the seventh generation from the days of Penn its most famous off-spring, Bayard Taylor, born at Kennett Square, in 1825, was as nearly German as Quaker, and it was the German blood, no doubt, which gave his nature its strain of poetry and romance.

The Taylor family were simple farmers, and the home life was plain, though the thrift of both father and mother secured the children every comfort. The mother's one desire was that her children should become quiet, respectable members of a community that their name had honored for generations. But to the fourth child, Bayard, this ambition always seemed narrow. His earliest memories of himself were connected with longings to flit as far beyond the home nest as possible.

At four years of age he became a reader of books, passing in due time from Peter Parley to Gibbon, and learning Scott and Campbell by heart, as well as copying long extracts from their works. Kennett Square possessed a public library, volume after volume of which was devoured by young Bayard. When he was seven years old he set himself gravely to the business of writing poetry, placing his own verses with much satisfaction among his copied extracts from the great poets.

Fond as he was of books, he was yet a genuine child, who delighted in playing tricks, and had a very real terror of a piece of lonely woodland that he had to pass through on his way to school.

He was an out-of-doors boy, too, and spent hours in swamp and field making collections of frogs and baby turtles, eggs, and mineralogical specimens. Among his other interests was a fondness for drawing. He illustrated his own little manuscript book of verses, and made pictures for the poems of his favorite authors. But his chief passion was a desire to travel.

Books of travel and descriptions of foreign lands were read and re-read and almost learned by heart. When called upon to write compositions at school he invariably chose for his theme some imaginary adventure in a strange country, or some fanciful description of a remote corner of the earth, whose name alone was familiar to him. Long afterward, in speaking of this desire of his childhood, he said that he envied the birds their wings, and would have given his life to make an ascent in a balloon.

His father had no sympathy with these boyish fancies. He intended to make a farmer of Bayard, and he scolded vigorously over his son's nonsensical ambitions. But farm service and farm life were distasteful to the boy. He often shirked his duties, and his mother frequently set him small tasks about the house, out of pity for his intense dislike of the work of field or garden.

When he was fourteen Bayard was sent to Unionville Academy, where he received his last and best school training from a competent and earnest teacher. He studied Latin, French, and mathematics, and among the young countrymen who came there for study he found two or three friends whom he kept for life.

When he was fifteen, with two of these friends he walked from Unionville to the Brandywine, noted as the scene of one of the famous battles of the Revolution. This little journey, the first flight of the boy into the world, made a deep impression upon him. More than ever he longed to breathe the air of wider skies, to learn the lessons taught by the art and history of the past, and to offer to the world's work some contribution, perhaps, which should not be valueless. He wrote a brief, but vivid, description of his little trip, which was published in the *Westchester Register*, a local paper of some repute. It was the first time he had seen his name in print, and its appearance thrilled him with hope.

A year later the *Saturday Evening Post*, of Philadelphia, printed his first published poem, "The Soliloquy of a Young Poet." Like Longfellow, he himself had carried his first offering surreptitiously to the newspaper office. As he read that the verses of "Selim," his pen name, had been accepted, he seemed to stand on air.

There is no more attractive picture of ambitious and noble youth than we get of Bayard Taylor at this moment. From childhood he had dreamed dreams far beyond the imagination of ordinary children. He had read poetry with his heart full of admiration for the men who could turn life to such golden uses. He gave the simple and innocent worship of his young soul to the famous authors who had taught him the meaning and riches of art. A letter which he received from Dickens in reply to one of his own brought him the greatest joy, and any whisper from the great world beyond his own delighted him.

At seventeen he finished his course at Unionville Academy and went back to the farm. But in his heart he was devoted to the literary life. From his own confessions we know how he consecrated himself to this work, cherishing a vision of high achievement and a hope that in the great march of life he might not be found laggard.

Winning his father's consent to his learning the printer's trade, he worked for two years in the office of *The Village Record*, of Westchester. During this time he studied Spanish, continued German, and wrote poems, which appeared in *Graham's Magazine*. But Bayard Taylor, while setting type in the office of *The Village Record*, was in spirit far away from the quiet Pennsylvania town, meditating voyages of discovery into new worlds, and when he published his first volume of poems, in the early part of 1842, the venture was a bid not so much for fame as for funds to start him on his travels.

The little book, under the title *Ximena ; or, the Battle of Sierra Morena, and other Poems,* was published by subscription. He sent copies to Lowell and Longfellow, whose approval he coveted, signing himself their "stranger friend." The book did not bring in money enough for a European journey. But the poet was young and strong and possessed indomitable perseverance. He had often walked the thirty miles that lay between his home and Philadelphia, and he felt that he could walk through Europe. At any rate, he meant to try it. After many disappointments he secured two or three engagements to write newspaper letters from abroad, receiving some pay in advance, and with this, added to another small store, he sailed for England, taking a second-cabin passage in July, 1844.

Now began as interesting and romantic a career as even our poet could have desired. Two friends joined him in his pilgrimage. Both were like Bayard Taylor himself, young, strong, and ambitious. When they caught sight of the Irish coast, after a voyage of nearly four weeks, it seemed to them that they had entered another world. Dressed in student's cap and blouse, with knapsack on back and pilgrim staff in hand, Bayard Taylor made the tour of Europe. Like a true vagrant, he wandered hither and thither as his fancy led him. For six months he studied German in Frankfort, living in the family of a burgher, and sharing with them their feasts and holiday merriment in true German fashion. Though poor in purse, he was not too poor to reciprocate their many kindnesses to him and his friends, and he tells a funny story of a Christmas gift bestowed upon their kind hosts. It was decided to make the worthy Germans a present of a carpet, such luxuries being unknown to the frugal household. The young students laid it down at night after the family had gone to bed, but in the morning they were somewhat dismayed to find that the housewife could not be induced to step upon it. It required much argument to persuade her that the gift was meant for service, and it is likely that she would have abandoned her

sitting-room while the carpet remained had not
the donors insisted upon its use.

From his strain of German blood, perhaps,
Bayard Taylor took more kindly to German
life and thought than to any other. As he
journeyed through the old picturesque towns,
and wandered by the banks of the rivers, that
had been famous since the times of Cæsar, he
felt fall upon him the spirit of romance and
mystery which seemed ever to brood over this
land. He loved the people with their simple
lives and solid intellectuality, and the legends
and stories which clustered around their mountains and forests seemed to come to him like
reviving memories of his own experience.

In the spirit of the old wandering bards he
made his way through the sombre forests of
the Hartz Mountains, and rejoiced like a
young viking that he was able to ascend the
Brocken in a raging storm.

All this time he was studying hard at German, preparing himself unknowingly for one
of the great labors of his life. All this time,
too, he was pressed for money. Travelling

through Austria, crossing the Alps, visiting Italy, he found it always necessary to earn his daily bread. Sometimes he lived on six cents a day, and thought bread, and figs, and roasted chestnuts sumptuous fare. Once his shoes were so worn that they would not bear him another step, and he had to wait five days at an inn until a letter came with remittances from his publishers. Again he was so poor that he could take only deck passage on the voyage from Italy to France, and made the trip with his knapsack for a pillow, drenched to the skin and suffering horribly from seasickness.

But he accomplished his desire. When he returned home, after a two-years' absence, he found that his letters in the New York *Tribune* and other papers had won him sufficient fame to warrant their publication in book form. N. P. Willis, the never-failing friend of young authors, wrote a preface, and *Views Afoot* came out under as pleasant auspices as could be desired, and passed through six editions in one year.

The appearance of this book marked the beginning of that larger literary life to which Bayard Taylor aspired and which he attained. A great and immediate satisfaction came to him now through friendly letters from older writers, who gave the book generous praise and welcomed the young author cordially to their guild. During a visit to Boston made at this time Bayard Taylor was overwhelmed with delight at the kind reception given him by Longfellow and the other men whose friendship he had always longed for. The publication of his poem, "The Norseman's Ride," a few months later brought him a letter from Whittier, and marked the beginning of a friendship which lasted through life.

After an unsuccessful attempt at publishing a county newspaper in Pennsylvania, Bayard Taylor decided to try his fortunes in New York.

The city still retained many of the characteristics which made it a congenial home for literary workers in the days when Irving and Bryant, Cooper, Halleck, and Drake were winning their fame.

The wealth and fashion still centred in the lower part of the town in broad, old-fashioned streets, whose houses were noted alike for their culture and hospitality.

New York then, as now, led the newspaper work of the country, and the younger writers were glad of positions on the dailies and week-lies. Bayard Taylor obtained a position on *The Literary World* at five dollars a week, and earned four dollars more by teaching in a girls' school. But he had already won a fair start in the literary field, and his friends looked on his success as assured. Their faith was realized; within a year Taylor was advanced to a position of twelve dollars a week on the *Tribune*, while writing articles for magazines.

From this time Bayard Taylor's literary life divides itself into that of traveller, newspaper writer, lecturer, novelist and poet.

Scarcely had he won his place in New York when he was sent by the *Tribune* to California to visit the newly discovered gold regions and report the life of the mining camps. Bayard Taylor was the prince of those literary free lances, the newspaper correspondents, who start on adventures as wild and full of danger as those encountered by knight or soldier of old. Civilization owes much to these men, always ready and full of pluck, and who count danger of small moment in pursuit of duty.

Bayard Taylor sailed from New York for California by way of the Isthmus of Panama, taking from June till August for the journey. He immediately threw his lot in with the miners, sharing their dangers and privations, and became the poet of the California emigration as Bret Harte afterward became its historian. He slept often on the ground with his saddle for a pillow, toiled through ravines, traversed forests, encountered Indians and wild beasts. In Mexico, on his return, he had an adventure with robbers.

But he had caught the spirit of that marvellous outburst of energy which in a few years transformed the thinly inhabited Pacific slope into a region of towns and cities, whose aggregated wealth was almost beyond credence. The record of what he saw, published under the title *Eldorado; or, Adventures in the Path of Empire*, was a picturesque and valuable contribution to the literature of the gold discovery.

The next year found him again upon his travels. This time he fulfilled an old dream by visiting the Orient. His excellence as a reporter of things comes from his power to merge his own personality in that of the people he met. As soon as he entered a foreign land he ceased to be Bayard Taylor, American traveller, and became Arab, Bedouin, or Turk, as the case might be.

On the Nile it seemed he must have lived always in Egypt, and he was served by his boatmen with peculiar reverence, as if they recognized in him a higher genius of their own race. In Damascus he dressed in the Syrian costume and smoked his pipe sitting cross-legged upon the roof-top. In Constantinople he wore even the Arab burnouse and turban, and was addressed in Turkish when he went to his bankers for money. At another time he was denounced as an infidel by an Arab who saw him drinking water on a fast-day. He himself rejoiced in the strange Oriental life, whose customs and habits of thought appealed to him so strongly. He called himself a worshipper of the sun, and says that standing in an Eastern garden of flowers he took off his hat to the god of day like a veritable Parsee. In India he became in spirit a Hindoo, and visited temples and shrines like a devotee. Still loyal to the mountain-tops, he climbed the highest point of the Himalayas accessible in the winter season, and drank in the solemn and majestic beauty of that region of mystery.

Under orders from the *Tribune*, he crossed Asia overland and joined the United States squadron at Shanghai, where Commodore Perry gave him the post of master's mate that he might witness the opening of the ports of Japan to the commerce of the world. Finally he sailed from China for New York by way of Cape Horn, reaching home two years and six months after his departure.

Three years later he was again on his wan-

derings. After a short visit in Germany he
started for the north and travelled through
Sweden, Denmark, and Lapland. He travelled
hundreds of miles by reindeer, penetrating far
within the Arctic Circle that he might enjoy
that wonder of the north, "a day without a
sun." A year after, he was in Greece breakfasting
on "honey from Hymettus," and began learning
Greek that he might better appreciate the mar-
vels of this land of beauty. In the same year he
visited Russia, returning to America in 1858.

After this, travelling occupied less of his
time, although he again made a tour of Europe,
and as a representative of the *Tribune* visited
Iceland during the celebration of its millennial
anniversary.

Iceland, the land of old memories and songs,
impressed him strongly. This little country,
which had preserved its national life for a
thousand years, had still the vigor of the old
viking days, when its sailors ventured without
compass or chart to the coasts of America, and
its poets sung its heroes' praises in verse that
has become classic.

Taylor's reputation had preceded him here, and he was called the "American Skald" by the enthusiastic people.

As a lecturer, Bayard Taylor's fame was based upon the widely diffused reports of his travels which had appeared for years in newspapers, magazines, and book form. He published thousands of letters and eleven books of travel, the most famous of these volumes including *A Journey to Central Africa; The Lands of the Saracen; A Visit to India, China, and Japan; Northern Travel,* and *Travels in Greece and Russia.*

Through these publications he had won a name which, in the intervals of life at home made him the most popular lecturer of his day. He delivered hundreds of lectures on his travels, his enormous capacity for hard work making this possible even in the midst of serious literary tasks. Moreover, he had been building up gradually a reputation as a novelist and poet. His first novel, *Hannah Thurston,* is an American story of manners, the characters of which are drawn from Pennsylvania life, although the scene is supposed to be laid elsewhere. This novel was successful in America, and appeared in German, Russian, and Swedish translations; but it is doubtful whether its fame was not due more to the author's popularity than to its own merit. The second novel, *John Godfrey's Fortunes*, was much more individual and characteristic. In this were incorporated certain experiences of the author's own literary life. There is a certain vitality about these reminiscences that will always make them agreeable reading. *The Story of Kennett*, the third novel, is the most interesting of all. It is largely a history of the village life of the author's boyhood, into which are woven many incidents of local history. The tricks which the Quaker boys play upon their sober-minded father and the account of the runaway match were family history, while the descriptions of scenery, the thousand memories of boyhood, and the tender handling of the subject all reveal the loyal affection in which the author held the past. One other novel, *Joseph and His Friend*, with some short stories contributed to *The Atlantic* and other magazines, sums up Bayard Taylor's work in fiction. While these novels were successful in their day, they are perhaps the least valuable of Bayard Taylor's work. His newspaper letters and his books of travel alike are full of that personal charm which made the author one of the most popular men of his day. They have, besides delightful touches of color and light, a ready *camaraderie*, and a genuine sentiment.

But neither in fiction nor tales of travel did the author aspire to the greatest achievement of his life. His boyish dream had been to be a poet, a younger brother of Goethe, and Shakespeare, and his best work is unquestionably his verse. Unequal though he is, yet Bayard Taylor possessed the true poet's gift. His chief fault lay in over-production. He wrote volume after volume of poetry which brought him reputation but not critical approval. His beauty-loving nature seemed to find poetry everywhere, and to demand its expression.

Much of his verse passes before the eye like

sunlit pictures. This is especially true of the *Poems of the Orient.* Here the traveller, charmed by his surroundings, has turned poet, and plucked from rose-garden and riverside a glowing wreath of song. The very breath of the Orient flows through these poems, which express a genuine inspiration. "A Boat Song of the Nile;" "An Arab Warrior;" "Kilimandjars; or, a Russian Boy;" "Desert Hymn to the Sun;" "The Arab to the Palm," and "A Bedouin's Love-Song" indicate by their titles the progress of the poet's pilgrimage through the lands whose romantic history had haunted his youth. In these and other ballads Bayard Taylor showed the temper of the genuine lyrist. Among the shorter poems "The Song of the Camp" has won a place in the heart of the people.

The longer poems embrace pastorals, tragedies, masques, and a drama. All show careful workmanship, for Bayard Taylor always approached his art with a feeling that it demanded the best that he could give. Many descriptive passages unvaryingly of great beauty are found scattered through this work, which is pure and lofty in conception. Among these longer poems "The Masque of the Gods" and "Lars, a Pastoral of Norway," are perhaps the most successful.

One of the great ambitions of Bayard Taylor was achieved in his translation of Goethe's *Faust*. To do this work he had for years studied every available source of knowledge. His familiarity with German was thorough, his sympathy with German thought complete. No man of his generation was so well equipped for the work, and he succeeded in producing a poetic, faithful, and spirited translation of the great original.

One other ambition, the writing of the life of Goethe, he was not allowed to accomplish. When apparently only in the midst of his career he died suddenly at Berlin, whither he had been sent as Ambassador from the United States. His early death was felt to be a serious loss to American letters, as his accomplished work seemed to promise still higher achievement.

Bayard Taylor's American home was for many years at Kennett Square, where he built a charming manor-house, noted for its hospitality as well as for the distinguished guests who visited it. He had a social and loving nature, and easily won and kept the friendships which he so dearly cherished. The poets Stoddard and Stedman were his lifelong intimates. His boyish desire to be admitted to the circle of men of genius found its realization in the place he held in the hearts of the greatest men of his day.

His other and higher youthful hope—to perform nobly his part in life—was also fulfilled. No man could have been freer from selfish and mean undertakings than was he. Whether in his literary work or in his diplomatic service he was ever guided by one principle—that life and its gifts were to be put to their best uses, and that the measure of noble purpose was the measure of the man.

CHAPTER VIII

WILLIAN DEAN HOWELLS

1837—

Perhaps the most faithful story of a boy's life ever written is given to us in *A Boy's Town*, a transcription of the home history of William Dean Howells, from his third to his eleventh year. The " Boy's Town " was Hamilton, O., whither the family had removed from Martin's Ferry, the birthplace of our author, and this picture of a Western town at that period has thus a unique value.

The greatest charm of this book is found in the utter absence of anything like an effort at story-telling proper. There are no hair-breadth escapes and few adventures, but one feels throughout the genuineness of this revelation of a boy's hopes and fears and ambitions. The narrative is in the impersonal form, and yet there is a fascinating *camaraderie* at once established between author and reader. " When I

was a child" is the note that sounds throughout, and this magic suggestion colors the story
with that reality which children love far beyond anything else.

These child pictures show us the home-life .
and the heart-life of the writer as nothing else
could. The family belonged to the well-to-do
portion of the community, the father being
perhaps better read than most of his neighbors. Both father and mother were wise in
the best sense for their children's good. Of
fun and frolic there was plenty, but there
was also the firm counsel to check all selfish-
ness and mean ambitions, to nourish regard for
others, and above all to teach right doing because it was right. Reading between the lines
we see that this father and mother, with their
high conceptions of duty and their constant example of earnest living must have moulded the
character of their children on broad and noble
lines.

There is a delightful little confession of how
the boy was once somewhat ashamed of his
father, because in the paper which he edited he

opposed the Mexican War. The leading people of Hamilton were in favor of the war and the children took sides in the issue. General Taylor, the hero of the hour, was the hero of the larger portion of the Hamilton boys, and Howells keenly felt the bitterness of unpopularity. But a little later he appreciated his father's bravery in battling day after day for a principle, though it made his paper unpopular and affected his business interests. When General Taylor was nominated for President, the paper strongly opposed his candidacy, because of his well-known sympathy with the cause of slavery. To favor the anti-slavery cause meant often to lose one's friends and position, yet the little paper became the organ of an anti-slavery crusade. Long before election day Howells had ceased to be ashamed of his father, and had come to admire his stalwart independence and his unselfish heroism in fighting for what he considered right. Such an example as this made home counsels a living creed and wrought in the children of the family a desire to bend life to high uses.

About this time Howells first heard the *Biglow Papers*, which his father read aloud as they came out in the Boston paper, and the famous Hosea became an intimate in the family, and there seems after this never to have been even the slightest distrust of his father's judgment.

From these pictures of home life we see the Hamilton of Howells's childhood as the typical Western town of the day which had not yet quite outgrown the period of frontier life. All around the town were log cabins, which served as the outposts of the unbroken forests beyond, and it was to the forests that the boys looked for their inspiration when thinking of the ambitions of later life. They were all de-termined to be—if not real Indians, since nature had so cruelly denied that—yet at least Indian hunters and slayers. Periodically, there were companies formed for the extermination of the red man, and the highest joy was to go off by themselves for a day's camping in the woods, and try to forget that they were the children of uninteresting, civilized white people. Howells began school when he was still very young, attending first a small private school, and later the public school of the town. Nothing occurred to him in his school-life of such importance as the amazing discovery that he could make poetry by rule. He found this out one day as he was fumbling the leaves of his grammar, and he accepted the statement that poetry could be made by rule just as solemnly and unequivocally as he would have accepted a similar statement in regard to magic. From this time he never ceased until he had mastered the rules of prosody—a word which, in itself, must have sounded like an incantation. He wrote verses with the most indefatigable zeal, and he had the uncommon joy of being able to see them in print, for standing upon a stool in his father's printing office, he set up the type himself, and, no doubt, watched the presses afterward with all the responsibility of ownership. Verse-making, which had often been tried before, now assumed a greater interest, and before very long the young author was busy upon a tragedy founded upon the

stern discipline of one of his school-teachers.
The teacher was to be the tyrant against whom
the boys were to revolt, much in the same way
as Spartacus and the gladiators revolted against
their Roman masters. The drama was finished,
but never acted by the school-boy company
selected for the parts. This, however, did not
discourage the young author, who still continued writing poetry.

A part of the family education consisted in
the father's reading aloud to the home circle in
the evening. In this way Howells became
acquainted with Moore's *Lalla Rookh*—which
was the first poem he ever remembers. Dickens's *Christmas Stories*, Scott's *Lady of the
Lake*, and some of the best English novels
became familiar to him at the same time. The
first books outside his school-books that he read
himself were Goldsmith's *Histories of Greece
and Rome.* A little later his father gave him
Don Quixote, and one of his literary ventures
was a romance founded upon the *Conquest of
Granada* as related in the pages of Irving, and
which he read over and over without tire.

In fact he was always reading, and from his very young boyhood he may be said to have been always writing; whatever other occupation or share of active duty became his, seems in his own mind to have been outside his real mission, which was that of writing. In this he persisted always, so that he may be said to have grown up into authorship.

Outside the home and school life were the never-ending and varied experiences of ordinary boy life. There were muster and election days, when the boys watched the soldiers drill with solemn joy, and straightway inaugurated military companies among themselves. There were Christmas holidays, which the boys celebrated, for some reason unknown to Eastern boys, with guns and pistols, firecrackers, and torpedoes. There were Easterday, when they cracked their colored eggs together in a game of win and lose; and April fools' day; and the annual May party, when the girls took the lead and the boys were content to play a secondary part; and Fourth of July celebrated with processions and

speeches and the usual noise. What would
have seemed strange to a New England
boy was the absence of any Thanksgiving Day,
of which Howells did not even hear the name
in childhood. Occasionally travelling shows
and circuses came to Hamilton, and sometimes a theatre company, and at such a time
the Howells children, owing to their father's
newspaper connection, were fortunate in being
provided with tickets that lasted throughout
these short seasons of joy. Besides these
amusements there were nutting and shooting
in the forest, fishing in the Miami River,
swimming in the canal and canal basins, and
the summer and winter sports in due season,
many of which held still that flavor of wildness
which suggested the early frontier life.

When Howells was ten years old he left
school and began to learn the printer's trade in
his father's office, and not very long afterward
the family removed to Dayton ; *A Boy's Town*
ends with an account of this removal, and a
pathetic little picture of how homesick Howells became for the old home. So homesick

8

indeed was he that there was nothing to do but let him return there for a visit, a remedy which cured him so effectually that he no sooner reached Hamilton than he started back for Dayton, possessed by a feeling even stronger than homesickness, and that was mother-sickness. At Dayton Howells and his elder brother helped with the new paper which their father had bought. They worked at the compositors' cases, and when it was sometimes necessary would rise early in the morning and help distribute the papers. Their education was carried on by their father in the evening, and he also superintended the reading in which the boys now indulged on a somewhat larger scale. One chief delight of the children at this period was the number of travelling theatre companies which visited Dayton; very often the best talent of the country was to be found among the strollers, and it was in this way that Howells became very well acquainted with the Shakespearean drama, and with old English comedy, as well as with the actors and actresses who had attained, or were destined to attain, an honorable celebrity. The Dayton home was a happy one, where the intellectual growth kept steady pace with the physical. But financially the paper was not a success, and the family was obliged to seek another home.

Howells and his father walked from Dayton to the new home, driving the cow and talking philosophy. This period of his life is preserved in Howells's charming book, *One Year in a Log Cabin*. It is a delightful transcription of the idyllic life of the woods. The little log cabin was almost as primitive as those built by the early settlers. The children helped the father cover the walls with newspapers and glaze the windows; the great open fireplace, where all the cooking was done and where the bread was baked in a Dutch oven set on the coals, was a new and delightful joy to them; so was the unbroken forest, around which still clustered memories of Indian warfare. At night these memories, mixed with the Indian tales which the boys read insatiably, made the bed-time hour one to be dreaded.

With true American indifference to circumstances the family life went on in the same
grooves. The manner of earning the living
was different, but the study and reading continued, the father still acting as teacher. In
his book, *My Literary Passions*, Howells has
told us the books that charmed him above all
others as a boy. These were Goldsmith's *History of Greece*, *Don Quixote*, and Irving's *Conquest of Granada*. As he read these books he
was for the time being an Alcibiades or Don
Quixote as the case might be. So powerful
was his sympathy with all heroic deeds that in
reading Irving he could never decide whether
he were Moor or Spaniard. His boy friends
—especially one who had worsted him in a
school-boy battle—had infinite respect for his
knowledge of the ancients and referred to him
for information with a deference that must
have been soothing. He says that later he
rather liked the Romans better than the
Greeks, because they were less civilized, and
more, in fact, like boys.

For the want of space a large part of the

family library still remained packed in barrels, and rummaging in these one day Howells came upon the poems of Longfellow. It was his first introduction to that poet, who was thereafter associated with the happy memories of this forest home. A life so close to nature left its own mark upon mind and soul, and this is seen in that rare quality, the idealization of childhood, which runs through the pages of *One Year in a Log Cabin.*

This glimpse of frontier life seen through eyes still young, has a charm like that of Longfellow's reminiscent poems of youth, or Whittier's transcriptions of his boyhood, in which the perfume of childhood still lingers around the deeper experiences of the man.

The log-cabin life gave place to newspaper work and another season in the printing office at Columbus. Between sixteen and seventeen a love for reading Shakespeare possessed Howells, and with a young friend, also given to verse making, he would spend afternoons in the country while they alternately read the tragedies and comedies of the great dramatist.

And so, although his education was desultory, by the time he was twenty he was well read in the English classics, and had besides a good knowledge of American literature.

Before very long Howells became known as one of the cleverest young newspaper writers of the West. He also began to publish verses in the newspapers. A trip down the Mississippi to St. Louis gave him a new experience of life, which he embodied in a poem, *The Pilot's Story*, a picture out of the history of slave life. This poem was published in the *Atlantic Monthly*, in which other poems from time to time appeared. About this time Howells published a book of poems, in which were included the verses of a young poet friend, and very slowly he began to gain a reputation for good verse making.

When Lincoln was nominated for President Howells was asked by a Columbus publishing house to write a life of the candidate. For this he received one hundred and sixty dollars, and he could conceive no better use for it than to enlarge his knowledge of the world. He accordingly made a trip to Montreal and Quebec, stopping, on his return, at Boston.

Here he became acquainted with James Russell Lowell, then editor of the *Atlantic*, with Oliver Wendell Holmes, and with other writers of note, who received the young author with kindness, and whose encouragement at that time was of the utmost value. In his twenty-fifth year Howells received from President Lincoln the appointment of United States Consul to Venice, where he lived for the next four years, making, in the meantime, trips to other places of interest, and familiarizing himself with Italian literature. The result of this experience is found in his charming book, *Venetian Life*, which was published in London in 1866, and in the volume, *Italian Journeys*, published in New York a year later. These two volumes mark the beginning of the serious work of Mr. Howells's life. Although only sketches of the every-day life of modern Italy, they are yet full of that peculiar quality which later was to stamp his fiction and give it a high place in American literature.

Upon his return to America Howells lived for a short time in New York, and did work for the *Times*, the *Tribune*, and the *Nation*. But being offered the assistant editorship of the *Atlantic Monthly*, he removed to Boston.

A pleasant summary of his experience as a resident of Cambridge is found in his book, *Suburban Sketches*.

He began his career as a novelist in 1871, and assumed the editorship of the *Atlantic* a year later. Since then his works have succeeded each other rapidly, his fame growing steadily from year to year. While busy with his novels he has found time to produce two volumes of verse, which include his earlier poems and those written since. In these poems, many of which show the finest poetic feeling, we have a new view of the successful novelist. Here may be seen his early susceptibility to natural scenes, as well as the more emotional side of his character. Some of these earlier poems are full of that reminiscent charm in which the hope, the ideality, and the unaccountable sadness of youth shine out with

tender grace. The later poems also are replete
with that susceptibility to feeling and impressions which can find fit expression only in
verse. All his poetry may, in fact, be said to
be transcriptions of those moods of mind
which come and go like day-dreams, and which
yet show the author's mind in a clearer and
truer light.

Some papers on Italian literature, the conduct of the Editor's Study in *Harper's Magazine*, and other miscellaneous work have run
side by side with the preparation of Mr. Howells's novels. Out of the numberless stories
told for the amusement of his children, he has
collected a dozen or so under the title *Christmas Every Day and Other Stories*, and made
a most charming contribution to juvenile literature.

Howells's gift above all others is to take
the ordinary occurrences of life and make
them interesting. To him the commonplace
appeals as a very large part of actual life, and
he has found his inspiration in dealing with
mankind at large rather than with unusual per-

sonalities or incidents. His theory is that
character and experience are the result of
growth, and of that slow growth which is built
moment by moment and day by day. Human
life thus running on from hour to hour presents to him a picture of the real struggles,
conquests, or defeats of the soul in the common relations of life, and his long series of
novels are but histories of the battles won or
lost by people whose experiences are never extraordinary but only such as are met by the
larger part of mankind. To him those rarer
idealizations which appeal to the genius of
Hawthorne or Poe are forced out of sight by
the actual contact with the many thousands
who march on monotonously day after day
and yet whose experience sums up the moral
achievements of the race.

This series of novels began with the publication of *Their Wedding Journey* in 1871, the
success of which determined Howells's career
as a novelist. This delightful little ending to
an old love story was followed by *A Chance
Acquaintance*, in which were incorporated some

charming impressions of Canadian travel.
None of the succeeding works has been cast
in quite so light a vein.

Throughout these character studies, which
now number many volumes, there runs the
earnest seriousness of the man who is in
sympathy with the aspiration, and yet whose
large charity can make him easily tolerate the
defects of mankind.

Sometimes the novel treats of the experience
of an individual and is the history of a commercial success, as in *The Rise of Silas Lap-
ham;* or of an intellectual struggle, as in *The
Minister's Charge ;* or of a crime, as in *The
Quality of Mercy;* very many of the later
works deal with those social questions which
are now under the consideration of every earnest thinker.

In his *A Traveller from Altruria* Howells
has treated one of these questions with unspar-
ing hand.   It is in these and similar books that
one sees the Americanism of the author and is
made to feel his interest in the highest welfare
of his native land.

Mr. Howells has in *The Mouse Trap and Other Farces* given us some delightfully humorous situations treated with all the delicacy of his art. In his *Modern Italian Poets* he has embodied the experience of twenty years' study of a century of Italian poetry, in a series of essays showing remarkable appreciation and insight. Some miscellaneous work in lighter vein shows still the genial fellowship which Howells always establishes between himself and his readers. With the exception of the different periods passed abroad, Mr. Howells has spent his life since leaving Ohio in Boston and New York, in which latter city he now lives.

The generous nature of the man is shown in his wide intercourse with his fellow-men in all grades of social life. His studies of human nature reflect always his own point of view, from which he sees man struggling ever with difficulties and discouragements, yet pressing patiently on toward higher levels.

CHAPTER IX

In the year 1866, a little girl left her birth-place in Manchester, England, and came to America to live. Her new home was in Eastern Tennessee, and thus her first impressions of America were connected with great mountain ridges reaching up to the sky, miles and miles of unbroken forest, and an unending succession of wild flowers which decked wood and stream with ever-changing beauty. These surroundings made the child supremely happy, for all her life she had longed for great out of door spaces to breathe in, great trees to play under, and flowers so plentiful that one could not count them; so the new home seemed enchanting.

Manchester, where her life had been theretofore spent, was one of the great manufacturing cities of England, and all day long the smoke from the tall factory chimneys hung over it and shut out the sky, while the streets were given up mainly to the dwellings of the operatives, or buildings connected with the commercial life of the place.   Here and there, however, were pleasant little squares and streets, where the people of the better class lived, and one of these squares had been the home of the child, Frances Hodgson, who, until she came to America, tried very hard to " make believe " that the trees in an English square represented a forest, that the clouds of smoke were real clouds, and that the rose-bushes, lilacs, and snowdrops of the garden opened into vistas of tropical bloom.

Many years after, when this little girl had become a woman and had children of her own, she wrote a book in which she put many pictures of this Manchester life; both the real world and the dream world, in which, like all imaginative children, she often wandered.   And here we learn that, as far back as she could remember, she was given to making up stories

—and, with the assistance of her dolls, acting
them in the privacy of the nursery—about
everything that she heard or read, or that in
any way touched her own life.

This naturally led to writing the stories
down as soon as her little fingers could man-
age it, and she seems to have had a very droll
time in trying to procure the paper so necessary for the work. Old exercise, or account
books, which still held a few pages untouched
by butchers' and grocers' accounts, were her
principal resource, and it was in one of these
she inscribed her first poem while she was still
such a little child that even the memory of
what it was about soon passed away from her.
Another poem, written on a Sunday evening
when the family were at church, she remembers better. It was a stormy evening, and she
started out to write a sad poem about loneliness, but her melancholy gave out at the end
of the first stanza, and with childish adapta-
bility she forthwith turned it into a funny
poem. It had enough cleverness to attract
some praise from her mother upon her return

from church, which so delighted the young
author that it laid a little seed of desire to do
still better things; it is possible that it was
this very little seed which grew and bloomed
at last into some very beautiful flowers of
literature. At any rate, from this time the
writing of stories went on quite indefatigably;
whether they won praise or blame the practice
must at least have been useful in developing a
power for sustained effort and a persistence
under difficulties, for outside the lack of paper
there was also the harsh and biting criticism
of two brothers, whose souls were devoted to
cricket and who thought themselves quite ill-
used in having a " romantic " sister.

But in her younger sister, Edith, and in a few
schoolmates, Frances found an audience which
would listen with delight to her tales, whether
written or told, from day to day in the intervals
of lessons. It is probable that these stories
showed little if any literary promise. They were
in the main tales of romantic lovers and sweet-
hearts, who bore a suspicious resemblance to
the heroes and heroines of Scott, Dickens, and

the novels published in *Blackwood's Magazine;* but their composition made an agreeable occupation for her active little mind,
and rendered her happy, and this was a great
deal.

After their removal to America, which was
brought about by the desire of the mother to
better the fortunes of her fatherless boys and
girls, Frances continued her story-telling and
story-writing, having still the sympathetic sister
as auditor. And one day when the two girls
were conjuring plans for helping the family
finances it suddenly occurred to the young
author to write a story and submit it for publication.

But this was a formidable task, for Frances
was absolutely sure that no editor would accept
a story not written on foolscap paper, and this
she neither possessed nor had the means of getting. Where could she obtain the money to
buy this paper? The sisters pondered and
pondered this difficult problem, and at last they
hit upon a joyful solution. Two little mulatto
girls whom they knew were making money

9

by gathering and selling the wild grapes which
grew in abundance in the neighboring woods.
Negotiations were entered upon with these
children, who promised to sell also the grapes
which Frances and her sister might gather. In
this way money was obtained for the foolscap
paper, and as that had been the most difficult
part of the business the story was soon dispatched to the magazine, with a modest note to
the editor telling him that the author's " object "
was "remuneration."

This venture was not entirely successful, the
editor of the magazine being willing to accept
the story but not to pay for it. Frances therefore asked for it back, and having still enough
grape money left to purchase the needed
stamps, she promptly dispatched it to another
editor. The story was a little romance of
English life, some of its scenes having actually
been written while the author still lived in
Manchester, and the new editor had some
doubts as to its originality. He therefore laid
a little trap for the young girl, and wrote to
say he would reserve judgment until he could

see another story from the same hand. Frances replied with a new story that was American in character, and this versatility seemed to convince the editor that he had really discovered a new story-writer; he sent thirty-five dollars for the two tales, and the girl's life as a fully fledged author began.

Other stories appeared rapidly during the next few years, and the reputation thus gained was greatly increased by the publication in 1872 of *Surly Tim's Trouble*, a dialect story. A year later the young author married and made a trip to Europe. Perhaps the home of her childhood thus revisited brought back early scenes with new force ; perhaps the memory of them had always lingered in the impressionable heart, at any rate the first great success of the author, now Frances Hodgson Burnett, came with the publication of *That Lass O' Lowrie's*, a story of Lancashire life. Years before, while still a little girl "making believe" that her real world was all that her dream world appeared, she had noticed, with a child's sharp intuitions, a certain factory girl who used sometimes to

wander into the square, and who somehow
seemed different from her companions. Although this girl was never "made into a story"
yet her personality lingered in the child's consciousness, and in later years stepped out from
the land of shadowy memories and became
the Joan Lowrie of the book. She was changed
from a millhand to a collier's daughter, and the
scene was laid in one of the English coal districts. It was the love story, pure and sweet,
of this uneducated girl of the mines and the
young overseer, whose position both as regards
birth and education was far above her own.
And it was told with such sympathy, such
directness and force, that it appealed to its
audience as a real story of actual life. The
author had indeed long since ceased to "make
up stories." Her imagination had become instead a magic lamp revealing to her the possibilities and experiences of the lives that touched
her own. Sometimes a little glimpse would
suffice to show her what lay behind, sometimes
two or three scenes would arrange themselves
so vividly as to indicate the whole drama, but

always at the bottom of the story could be seen
a foundation of truth.

In *That Lass O' Lowrie's* the colliers speak
that Lancashire dialect which Mrs. Burnett had
learned surreptitiously as a child, either by
listening to the factory people as they passed
the gates of the square in which she lived, or
by stolen visits to their homes in the back
streets. The dialect and its idioms had a fascination for her; she and some of her little
friends learned it with much greater enthusi-
asm than they devoted to their French, and
when no one was listening they held long conversations and talked as the "back street" people talked. It was an accomplishment that
served well in after years, and Mrs. Burnett's
power for the picturesque reproduction of
scenes unfamiliar to her readers is no doubt due
in some measure to her self-training of ear and
eye in her old life at Manchester.

Another interesting story of English life is
Haworth's, in which the hero is one of those
dreamers of dreams, lucky enough to realize his
ambitions. One or two of the characters in

this book give Mrs. Burnett an opportunity to indulge in that delightful sense of humor which lights nearly all her work, and which shows her keenly alive to the comedy of life.

Perhaps her touch is nowhere more faithful than in her story of American life, *Through One Administration*. And in *A Fair Barbarian* she shows an equal power of picturing the contrasts of American and English life.

In her charming juvenile book, *Piccino*, Mrs. Burnett tells how *Little Lord Fauntleroy*, her first phenomenally successful child's book, "grew." It was really a life study of her own little boy, whose sweet and merry disposition, thoughtful sayings, and infantile wisdom made him the delight of the house. His odd little views of American and English life suggested to her the idea of a story in which a little American boy should be brought into contact with aristocratic English life. How well she succeeded is evinced by the enormous circulation of the book, which went through edition after edition, and by its adaptation into one of the most successful dramas of childhood.

Giovanni and the Others is in itself a collection of beautiful stories of childhood, with whose dreams and hopes Mrs. Burnett is always in such loving sympathy.

An ideal child's book is *Sara Crewe*, the story of a little orphan girl whose miseries are turned to joys by fairy fortune. This small heroine is one of the most fascinating of the author's productions. She is so real, so pathetic, so much a simple, ordinary little girl, perplexed with the troubles that often visit the young, yet bearing through it all that infinite child faith in goodness and love.

Little St. Elizabeth, Piccino, and *Two Little Pilgrims' Progress* are also interpretations of the child mind. In all her work it is this power of sympathy which moves her to the highest efforts of her art. In that charming autobiography of her childhood, *The One I Knew the Best of All,* the reader is struck by this note of sympathy which sounds in her earliest recollections. Whether at play in the garden, or perched upon

the shelf of the old " secrétaire," reading tales
out of *Blackwood*, or listening to the factory
people in the back streets, or weaving romances
for the amusement of her little friends, the child
was always for the moment intensely alive to
the situations she had created.   She lived thus
in many worlds, moved among many scenes
strange to her own experience, and learned
early that one of the best things in life is to
forget one's own self in the experiences of
others.

This power of self-forgetting, this art of wandering through realms of thought unknown to
actual touch, are the chief factors that make
Mrs. Burnett's productions living characters,
whose interests fascinate, and whose fortunes
become for the time our own.

Mrs. Burnett calls Washington her home,
but she also lives much abroad.   One great
sorrow of her life was the loss of her son Lio-
nel, the older brother of Little Lord Fauntleroy.   Perhaps it is this which has touched some
of her work for children with a subtle sadness.
This has found its best expression, however,

in the desire to give practical aid to the many boys whose fortunes have been less fair than those of her own sons, and who owe much to her generous sympathy with their need. It is a pleasant thought that this dark shadow should have turned into the sunshine which has lighted many young lives that without it would have been shadowed too.

CHAPTER X

One of the functions of literature is to record the story of the home life of a nation. In the United States this life has developed under very varied conditions, and the stories of East, West, and South all differ widely from one another. New England society was made up of different elements from those which composed that of the Southern plantation or the Western mining camp; yet the picture of each community is interesting and valuable.

Among the most interesting of these stories of social conditions are those relating to the South. Here many different pictures are presented, and American literature has been fortunate in being able to have them transcribed at first hand.

This has been done by the men and women

whose memories go back beyond the war, and yet who were still young when the South began that great effort of rebuilding, which has made its recent history one of such splendid achievement. These stories of the South before and immediately after the war could only have been written by Southerners. Every word and incident, every scene and finished picture, is full of that child love which only the native born can feel ; the same love which sacrificed all in the dark days of the war, and which still cherishes with passionate devotion the memory of the past.

Under such inspiration the literature of the new South comes to us full of tender meaning. Its writers give to us the recollections that are most sacred to them, and we have in them not only a picture of Southern life, but a revelation of the heart. All the broken, childish memories of plantation songs, folk-lore tales, and negro superstitions that floated in the mind for years are here crystallized into form, and make a record of vital and enduring value.

Much of this literature has been thrown into

the form of the short story, and among the most delightful of these writers is Colonel Richard Malcolm Johnston, the historian of the " crackers," or poor white people of middle Georgia. Colonel Johnston was born in Hancock County, Ga., in 1822. His father was a large planter, and his earliest years were spent upon the farm. This life differed in many ways from the usual life of the plantations. Usually the poor whites of the South were looked down upon and despised because of their ignorance, poverty, and shiftlessness. But in the regions of middle Georgia the conditions were different. The poor white was still ignorant and shiftless, he was often lazy, and he was never very successful, but in some way he managed to make himself respected. The life of the planters here was very simple. Their children played with those of their poor neighbors and negroes, and in this happy community of interests young Richard spent the most impressionable years of his life. His intimates were the little black and white children, who, though different in birth, knew as well as he the secrets of wood and stream. With them he set traps, fished, played games, went to mill, and shared his holiday joys and presents. When some wandering master would open a school for a few weeks in the neighborhood, Richard would attend hand in hand with the little "crackers." Together they struggled over reading, writing, and arithmetic, and when the teacher was surly and unjust, as often happened, they endured together his harshness and cruelty.

In this atmosphere the boy learned to know the fine elements of character that often lay beneath the rough exterior of his poorer neighbors; here too he imbibed that sweet and broad humanity which breathes through all his work and makes it seem the presentation of a nature exceptionally noble.

In his series of stories called *The Dukesborough Tales*, Colonel Johnston has described one of those country temples of learning so familiar to his childhood. *The Goose Pond School* is a memory of one of those ill-conditioned creatures who, under the pretence of teaching, made miserable the lives of the ten or twenty children committed to their charge. Happily this specimen of instructor was rare, even in Colonel Johnston's youth, when corporal punishment was thought so essential to good discipline. This story, containing so much tenderness and sympathy, is a revelation of the heart of the boy who treasured it so many years. The picture of the little hero struggling with injustice, disgraced in the sight of his mates, and yet enduring it all bravely for the sake of his mother, shines out in the bright lights which the author loves to throw upon the character of the humble " cracker."

Another reminiscence of youth is found in *The Early Majority of Mr. Thomas Watts*, the scene of which is laid in Powelton, whither Colonel Johnston's family had removed. Powelton had an excellent school conducted by a staff of New England teachers. Boys and girls sat together and learned the same lessons, and Richard Malcolm Johnston was one of the most promising pupils, and began here the serious study for that ripe scholarship which he attained. The types of character which

abounded in Powelton have passed into literature, *The Dukesborough Tales* being but so
many transcriptions of the different personalities found in this little hamlet of one hundred
and fifty inhabitants. It is evident that the
.boy who was studying mathematics and Latin
so diligently, who was first on the playground
and the leader of all boyish escapades, was beyond this a student of his fellow-beings. *The
Dukesborough Tales* could only have been
written by one familiar from childhood with
the originals. For beside the art which gives
them a high place in literary composition, they
are full of the flavor of the soil.

From Powelton Johnston went to college,
and after he was graduated studied law. For
ten years he practised in the circuits of northern and middle Georgia, travelling from court
to court, much in the same way that the circuit preachers of the West discharged their
duties. It was an experience full of charm for
the young lawyer who always found human
nature so interesting. Many funny incidents
relieved the monotony of the law business,

while constant companionship with the country people made a valuable study for their future historian. The circuit lawyer, like the circuit rider, has now passed away; but his picturesque figure is preserved in the records of Colonel Johnston's memory, and his likeness, traced amid his unique surroundings, has found a permanent place in our literature.

In 1851, in his thirtieth year, Colonel Johnston accepted the professorship of *belles lettres* in the State University of Maryland. Four years later he started a boys' school at his plantation, where he endeavored to put in practice certain ideas which he held of broader education. He was over fifty years old when he began writing those stories of Georgia life which have made him one of the leading writers of the South.

But his whole life had been really an education for this work. He had had a soldier's training in the field of fiction—the practical experience, and the hand to hand touch with the life he described. All his characters are genuine. He lived with them as boy and man, and he knew their hearts as only such a close companion could. This absolute fidelity to nature, combined with the finest artistic perception, makes of these stories *genre* pictures of rare value. They are, moreover, touched by that homely love which shows the artist native born.

Almost with the first presentation of this life Colonel Johnston became famous. His stories succeeded each other rapidly, and the several collections of them have an assured place. *The Dukesborough Tales; Mr. Absalom Billingsbee and Other Georgia Folk; Two Gray Tourists,* and others of the series alike illustrate the author's happy gift for producing unique and picturesque character studies.

Besides his work in fiction, Colonel Johnston has written, in conjunction with a friend, a history of English literature; he is also the author of a life of Alexander Stephens, a biography of great value. His genial personality pervades all his work, and makes the kindly humor, the generous heartiness, and the exqui-

site sympathy but a reflection of his own rare
nature.

Among the children who walked the streets
of New Orleans immediately after the war,
and noted the changes that were rapidly trans-
forming the old city, was one bright-eyed girl
who was destined to become one of its most
interesting historians. Born of mixed Irish
and Southern blood, she had inherited from
both races the qualities that go to make up
the story-teller. The everyday, yet constantly
changing scenes of her childhood were picturesque and wonderfully interesting, for New
Orleans, above all others, was the city of contrasts.

In the French quarters still dwelt the aristocratic Creole families, descendants of the
original settlers, who had retained for generations the traditions of the French race. In
the business portion could be seen the typical
Irish and Yankee face mingling with the
Southern American. Along the wharves and
in the market the Italian emigrants vended

their wares, and everywhere swarmed the negro, the birthright of the old city, since the beginning of slavery.

Long after the girl had reached womanhood, the recollections of home and street and school still remained vivid, and ever more and more they began to weave stories in her mind. At first she was hardly conscious of this, it seemed so much like the old pictures of her childhood which had come and gone at will; but by and by the characters in the stories began to say and do things quite independently, as if they were real people, and at last, because they seemed to insist upon it, they were written down.

They were none of them exactly true stories, being nearly all made up of different scenes fitted in together, but they were exact pictures of the life of New Orleans as the author had seen it, and in this they had a value all their own.

Lying close beside these impressions were others of maturer years, spent in the country districts of Arkansas, among those village types

which are as curious and interesting in their
way as the typical New England villagers.
And presently, these unique personalities
stepped out from the shadowy fields of memory, and also began weaving stories about
themselves. As in the case of the others,
they were not exactly true stories, yet they
were all things that actually happened, or
might have happened, in the lives of the Arkansas country folk, and they verified the old
adage that no life can really be, or seem to be,
humdrum, if but the proper observer appears
to record it.

It was inevitable that these stories should
also be written down, and gradually they
began to appear in the different periodicals.
They were well liked, and by the time they
had grown into bulk for a volume, their author, Mrs. Ruth McEnery Stuart, had won a
name as one of the most interesting local historians of the South.

The stories which deal with the street
scenes of New Orleans and with old plantation life are full of color and picturesque

effect, and they are all vividly true to life.

Whether Mrs. Stuart is describing an Italian fruit vender's booth, as in *Camelia Riccardo*, or the little bare hut of an old negro, as in *Duke's Christmas*, each touch is faithful to the life; there is, moreover, in the tales of negro life that same subtle blending of humor and pathos which characterizes the race itself, and makes of the little sketches genuine life history.

A Golden Wedding, a story of a man and his wife who were separated before the war and only re-united in old age, is one of those pathetic memories of slavery transcribed with a loving sympathy which wins the heart, while the author is equally ready to enter into a relation of the violent flirtations of the *Widder Johnsing* or the desperate courtship of *Jessekiah Brown*. Not the least valuable thing about these stories is their reminiscent suggestion of many phases of negro life that must inevitably soon pass away. The bits of local color, the poetic yet crude imagination, the careless jollity and the childlike abandon of spirits all belong to the negro as he was before the war, when he was an irresponsible, fun-loving, yet often pathetic figure. With responsibility, education, and the dignity of freedom, the old life must at last pass, and it has been a task full of rich result to thus preserve the old plantation traditions of this picturesque race.

In her delineations of Arkansas country life Mrs. Stuart is equally happy. Perhaps she reaches the highest point in her work in *The Woman's Exchange of Simpkinsville*, wherein is told with tender reverence the story of a man who devoted his life to science, never dreamed of fame, who died unknown, and yet who left behind him a finished work so beautiful in scope that it placed his name high in the list of those who labor for the world's good. *Bud Zundt's Mail*, and *Christmas Geese* must also be reckoned among the best of these stories of Arkansas life.

In her stories of negro life Mrs. Stuart's work has a distinctive note not found in that of any other Southern writer. The picture is always taken from the negro's point of view, and thus reflects many interesting side lights. The pathos and humor, tragedy and childlike lightheartedness are always presented in natural proportions in these sketches of the experiences of the race whose history has been so unique, and shining through them all is ever seen that subtle sympathy with the situation which is the mark of the Southern blood. The chronicler is always the foster child of the cabin who brings her gift of art and lays it with loving grace into the black hands whose tender ministry formed her earliest recollection.

Mrs. Stuart's third book, *Babette*, is the story of a little creole girl who was stolen from her parents and who grew to womanhood before she was restored to her family. This little story contains many charming features necessarily absent from Mrs. Stuart's other work. The description of the *Mardi Gras*, and of the miserable Italian settlement where Babette lived with the old woman who stole her, the little pictures of creole family life, and the local setting, are all vivid reproductions of the scenes familiar to the New Orleans of

the author's youth.   Of less artistic value than
the other work, the romance of *Babette* is yet
warm with the colors of youth, pluck, and fine
ambition.

Among her other juvenile work, *Solomon
Crow's Christmas Pocket*, a Christmas tale
with a picturesque little negro for the hero, will
always hold a high place.   *Lady Quackelina*,
the history of a duck whose eggs were exchanged, and who, to her great consternation,
hatched out twenty small guineas, is another of
this author's happy conceits.

Quackelina had the good fortune, however,
to have her legitimate children restored to her,
as they were wandering away from their foster-
mother, the guinea-hen.   The little odd turns
of thought peculiar to ducks and guinea-hens
are here translated by Mrs. Stuart with the
felicity that shows her facile talent at its best.

The Two Tims, another Christmas story, is
full of that subtle pathos which clings to all
her studies of negro character.   Old Tim, the
grandfather, is rich in the possession of a banjo
that was " born white " and had been played on

with "note music" by its former master. The relation of how old Tim came to share this priceless treasure with young Tim makes up the story, which is one of the sweetest and tenderest to be found in the author's work.

Other stories of children, some miscellaneous matter that has appeared in periodicals, and several delicate, beautiful studies of Arkansas folk-life, comprise the rest of Mrs. Stuart's contribution to literature, while her pen is still busy with the preparation of other work.

No one can tell just when that delightful relative, Brer Rabbit, entered upon the career which has made him famous. It is more than probable that under different aliases he figured in the household life of nations so old that they might be styled the great-great or even fairy grandmothers of the American Union. Of this we are not quite sure. But we know that the African, to whose simple mind the whole animal creation seemed big and little brothers, guarded Brer Rabbit's claims with loving fidelity. They enshrined his deeds in their unwritten history, and when the days of slavery began they brought him with them across the sea and gave him a place of honor in their humble cabins. Here for generations the story of his adventures delighted the children of the South, and we can never be sufficiently grateful to Joel Chandler Harris for giving it literary form.

This prince of biographers learned the story of his hero from the lips of the old colored uncles and mammies who were the historians of the plantation. Learned scholars have since that time tried to find the sources of this curious history, but they have not been very successful. They only know that through the changes of centuries, during which time the African lost his nationality and language, he has kept these legends and superstitions in his heart.

These folk-lore tales which thus cling to the mind of a race are as much a part of it as its physical characteristics; they are often the only records of its early history, and as they drift down the stream of time they become valuable mementoes of the far-off days of a people's beginning. The American slave guarded the legend which was still cherished by his brother in Africa, but the memory of its meaning had long since faded from his mind. But Mr. Harris, by collecting these stories, has still done valuable work for the scholar, while to literature he has added new treasures.

Joel Chandler Harris, like Colonel Johnston, is a native of Georgia. He was born at Eatonton in 1848, and as a very young child he confesses to a desperate ambition to write something that might appear in print. This innocent desire he expressed so freely that his fellow-townspeople could not help becoming interested in its fulfilment. A boy who wished to write was a phenomenon in Eatonton, where the juvenile mind inclined to less ambitious pleasures, and young Harris was looked at by his associates very much as they would have regarded an Arctic traveller, or a visitor from Japan. Still he was a genuine boy, and outside of his inclination toward literature, his companions had no cause to distrust

the ambition which was as distinctly toward
fun as they could desire. Harris was the
leader in boyish escapades and adventures, and
none the less a true leader because his mind
sometimes took flights far beyond the horizon
of daily life.

His wish to write was fostered by a little
incident which thrilled his soul with delight.
A " real editor," who had learned somehow of
the boy's aspirations, gravely presented him
one day with a copy of his paper. Harris felt
as if he had received his commission, and what
romance of the future he wove around this
trifling circumstance only the imagination
of boyhood can understand.

When he was fourteen life seemed to shape
itself toward the attainment of his desire. A
paper called *The Countryman* was started on
the Turner plantation, near his home, and an
apprentice to learn printing was desired.
Harris saw the advertisement, and flew to
the office, where his eagerness and his un-
qualified promise to devote himself to the
work secured him the engagement.

Now began an ideal existence for the boy, who by this time had grown into a student. Books were rare in the Harris home, but at the Turner plantation there was a valuable private library, and to this the young apprentice had free access. He read like one who was reading for a prize; and in this flight into the intellectual world it seemed that his spirit was finding its true element. His childish ambition to write something for print now appeared to him to have a meaning; it was with joy that he applied himself to the practical details of his work, feeling it a means to a higher end.

The printing office was in the woods, where came many uninvited visitors with tempting offers of recreation. Blue jays swung in the trees and scoffed at work; woodpeckers hammered upon the roof; squirrels played upon the window-sill and pretended that the gathering of winter stores was no part of their existence. What boy could withstand such temptations? Harris could not. He was in the main a faithful apprentice, but many an hour

was spent in the wood haunts of these wild
children of the forest. Here he learned wood
lore and became skilled in the interpretation
of bird song and squirrel chatter; here it
seems he must have become familiar with
those ·fascinating, human-like traits of animal
character which he has transcribed so faithfully in his work.

This shows that he was a student of other
things than books, and presently his mind took
another and. still wider outlook. He associated
much with the country people who lived in the
neighborhood, and very often accompanied
them in fishing trips and hunting expeditions
to the mountains. Without knowing it he
now became a student of human nature, and
thus gained the knowledge that could best fit
him for a literary career. The picturesque side
of this life appealed to him as well as the
deeper meaning which lay beneath its commonplace ambitions and struggles; no phase
of it seemed uninteresting, and the insight and
experience so acquired became potent factors
in his education. Study from books still went

on ; by the light of his knot-wood fire he spent long hours over history, biography, and poetry. The widest knowledge forms the best training for the specialist, and unconsciously Harris was receiving that liberal education which makes his *Uncle Remus Stories* such minute and faithful revelations of animal character that it seems Brer Rabbit himself must have been the scribe.

The war put an end to this happy existence. The Turner plantation lay along the route of Sherman's march to the sea, and the printing-office went out of existence. Harris, however, kept firm hold of his purpose, and almost immediately after the close of the war entered the office of the *Savannah News* as associate editor. He had determined to devote himself to newspaper work, and for this he trained himself as thoroughly as opportunity offered. It was characteristic of his mind that his chosen calling should seem an end in itself and not merely an introduction to the literary life. His editorial work was from the beginning conscientious and scholarly. It was the outcome of a brain which saw clearly the accomplishment that might lie in this field, and from first to last it thrills with the fine purpose and masterful energy of the ideal newspaper editor.

After he had become editor of the *Atlanta Constitution*, Harris conceived one day the idea of transcribing one or two of those folk-lore stories which he had heard so frequently from the lips of the negroes. The result took the form of the first two of the *Uncle Remus Stories*, and as an experiment he printed them in his paper. The reception they met surprised him. Uncle Remus seemed at once to step into the place which the ages had prepared for him. His chronicle, like other long-neglected fragments of old-world lore, had been drawn at last into the great stream of literature, and had become history. Scholars recognized the value of this new gift to folk-lore literature, and welcomed each succeeding story with delight, while the popular taste made of Uncle Remus a favorite hero.

By the time the stories had grown into a volume, critic and laymen alike appreciated the debt that American literature owes the South for the preservation of these charming legends. Mr. Harris's gift as a writer has made of these stories almost perfect pieces of art. · The skill with which he effaces himself, and makes Uncle Remus the real narrator is marvellous. This old time, consequential, but delightful product of plantation life, dominates the series, and relates the adventures of Brer Rabbit with all the respect of the genuine historian for a favorite character. Interwoven with the legends are those innumerable reflections of the negro character which show their jollity and homely wisdom in the most charming light. We might have learned from some other source why the guinea - fowls are speckled, but only Uncle Remus himself could have woven into the narrative those threads of shining recollection which show the very warp and woof of the author's brain. *Brother Fox's Fish Trap ; The Moon in the Mill Pond;* and *Why Mr. Possum Loves Peace,* are other expressions of the African's appreciation of the animal cunning which he himself largely possesses. Equally full of the personal element is the delightful *Story of the Little Rabbits*, an irresistible appeal to the child-mind, which sees in all young things a likeness to itself. *Mr. Rabbit and Mr. Bear*, and *How Brer Rabbit Found His Match at Last*, are among the most fascinating adventures of our hero, who retains his place in the reader's heart even though overmastered by cunning greater than his own.

These stories have all now been successfully produced in book form. Mr. Harris considered their preparation as incidental, and emphatically pronounces his work to be that of journalism. But he has created an artistic success that our literature could not well spare.

The personal history of F. Hopkinson Smith, one of the most popular of Southern writers, is the story of pluck. Long before he ever thought of writing he had laid his life out on other lines, and had wrested success out of many disheartenments. Mr. Smith says that the secret of his success in painting,

writing, and civil engineering, is the result of
the severe application of his motto—*work,
work, work,* and that indomitable perseverance has alone made accomplishment possible.

He was born in Baltimore, in 1838, of an
old Virginia family, and his early years were
spent in that atmosphere of refinement and
good living which obtained in the Southern
home. He was an active boy, fond of fun,
and a leader in the amusements which cheered
the open-hearted hospitality of the family life.
The old-fashioned house was dominated by
the spirit of his mother, a remarkable woman,
to whom everybody turned for advice, and
who was called "the oracle" by relatives and
friends alike. The mother and son were companions and comrades, in the fine sense of the
word. To her he turned for sympathy in his
boyish interests, and it was her beneficent influence which shaped the ambitions of his manhood. He took lessons in drawing from an
old artist, giving up his Saturday holidays to
learning the secrets of the art he loved so well.
Drawing, reading, and study, however, all gave

place occasionally to pure fun, when he would play practical jokes upon the old-time watchmen who had charge of the Baltimore streets, or lead his companions in the mischievous escapades which originated in his own fertile brain.

Hopkinson was prepared for Princeton College by the time he was sixteen, but a change in the family fortunes made it necessary for him to abandon a college career and he entered a hardware store as a shipping clerk, at a salary of one dollar a week. After various experiences in business life Mr. Smith became a contractor, and furnished material for the construction of government buildings along the coast. And not very long after he became a civil engineer. Mr. Smith did not take a course at any school of technology to fit him for his new duties. His art was entirely self-taught, but he had a background of practical experience that made invaluable training.

His first work in his new profession was to build a stone ice-breaker around the light-house at Bridgeport, Conn. Since then Mr. Smith has built light-houses, sea-walls, life-saving stations, and other government coast buildings, his field of work ranging from end to end of the Atlantic seaboard. The work of which he is most proud is the Race Rock Light-house off New London. He was six years in building this light-house, the situation being so difficult to conquer that more than once it seemed that it must be abandoned. The foundation had to be laid far beneath the waves, and often storm and sea combined to undo the patient efforts of months. Mr. Smith almost lived on the rock with his men, and when a terrific storm would arise and the structure was in danger he only became more resolute, though he knew the work of a whole year might be swept away in a single night. He says that the Race Rock Light-house made him; out of this effort had come a faith in the power of persistent effort which nothing could ever efface. One of Mr. Smith's most interesting pieces of engineering, was the laying of the foundation of the statue of Liberty enlightening the world in New York Harbor.

During these busy years of active, practical out-of-door life Mr. Smith was busy at spare moments with pencil and brush. Gradually he won for himself a reputation for his water-color drawings, and for fifteen years he spent every August in the White Mountains studying from nature. Travel in the West Indies, Mexico, and Europe, completed his education for the life of the artist. Of late years he has spent nearly every summer in Venice, whose picturesque beauty he has reproduced over and over again with faithful touch.

His literary life is an outgrowth of his work as an artist. During the publication of a reproduction in book form of a series of his water-color drawings the publisher wrote and asked Mr. Smith if he could not supply some brief descriptions of the points illustrated. In compliance with this request the artist wrote the sketch *The Church of San Pablo;* which formed the initial number of the series of interesting sketches published under the title *Well-worn Roads*, the author's first book. During the ten years following its appearance,

Mr. Smith has won an honest fame for artistic literary production. Much of his work has been descriptive of the places which he has visited, but in the domain of fiction he has also been a successful adventurer. True to the instinct of the Southern writer, Mr. Smith has given us as his masterpiece one of those rare pictures which illustrate life in the South. From memory and experience he gathered the elements which made up the character of a Southern gentleman of the old school, and presented, in *Colonel Carter of Cartersville*, a picture so faithful that it is worthy of rank as a family portrait. The motive of the story revolves around the continual difficulties which beset the old gentleman because he cannot remember that what is bought must be paid for. The book abounds in graceful and humorous situations, and the character of Colonel Carter, always honorable and high minded, shines luminous to the end. The success of the book led to its dramatization ; and its success as a piece of artistic light comedy has abundantly illustrated its dramatic possibilities. ·

Mr. Smith has not, however, confined himself to the representation of Southern life. *Tom Grogan*, next to *Colonel Carter*, his most important work, is a spirited and valuable piece of portraiture, whose original was found among the force employed in building the sea-wall around Governor's Island. Here, among his gang of laborers, the author found the cheerful, capable Irishwoman who is the heroine of the book. The story is full of the sympathy with human nature which Mr. Smith's experience as a leader and director of other men's actions has so largely developed.

Like Joel Chandler Harris, Mr. Smith considers his literary career as almost incidental. He says that he is a civil engineer, who is lucky enough to find time to devote to literature and painting. But the character of his work shows the temper of the true artist, who serves art for its own sake, and who is willing to bring to the service his most earnest devotion.

No part of the South shows more interesting social conditions than the region of the

Tennessee Mountains. Here, where for so many years the settlers were remote from the rest of the world, they developed tastes and interests widely different from those of Southern city and plantation life.

The daily life of these people was simple in the extreme. While the East was building great manufacturing and commercial interests, the South developing the luxurious life of the plantation, and the West pouring its resistless energy into the mining of gold and silver, the dwellers of the Tennessee Mountains still kept to the primitive habits of early frontier life. The men hunted, fished, and tilled the soil only as strict necessity required. The women wove and spun, the mothers and daughters performing all the household duties. The girls were taught only the simplest home tasks, while each boy was trained into such a knowledge of wood lore, hunting, and shooting as would have delighted the heart of Daniel Boone.

The life in the main was that of a community whose interests are one. No one was rich, yet in these little homes, barely furnished and unattractive, no one thought himself poor. Hospitality abounded, and each gave to the other's need with a generosity that knew no touch of either patronage or shame.

But however simple it may be, the life of every people is full of events which make up home histories and heart histories; there came a day when the Tennessee Mountains found their chronicler, and as seemed most right, the chronicle was written by one who was mountain born.

This was Mary Noailles Murfree, who was born at Grantlands, the family home near Murfreesboro, named after her ancestor, Colonel Murfree, of Revolutionary fame. Miss Murfree made her studies of Tennessee life from nature. Her childhood was spent among the people whose humble lives she describes with the loving fidelity of a native historian. Though well-born and tenderly reared, her heart, educated by contact with these mountaineers, responded generously to their unaffected worth.

She saw that here survived a race which still held many traditions of the young days of the republic, when communities were welded

together by common interests, and where simplicity of living very often bred largeness of
nature.

Under the often uncouth exterior of these
men and women she found the most generous
hospitality, the delicacy of sincere good fellowship, and the inborn self-respect that made the
mountaineers genuine lords of the soil. She
saw, too, the finer graces that lay like bloom
upon these rough lives. In her lovely sketch
of girlhood—*The Star in the Valley*—one
sees the flower-like innocence and charm of
the young heroine shining out amid her sordid
surroundings, while her story of self-sacrifice
appeals to the heart.

Again and again this note of human sympathy, sweet as a wild bird's song, and with as
legitimate a place in the great harmonies of
life, thrills through these vivid transcriptions.
Sketch after sketch presented itself to the
author's mind, was written down and published, and in 1884, a volume of the stories
appeared under the title, *In the Tennessee
Mountains.*

Miss Murfree's work appeared from the beginning under the pseudonym, Charles Egbert Craddock, and she had won fame long before her personality was discovered. All her stories, now numbering several volumes, have been published under her pen name. The titles of the books—*Where the Battle was Fought; Down the Ravine; The Prophet of the Great Smoky Mountains; In the Clouds; The Story of Keedon Bluffs; The Despot of Bloomsedge Cove;* and *His Fallen Star*, all show their local setting, and are interesting as being stories of the home life of a people still in the primitive stage of its existence. The Tennessee mountaineer will lose his individuality with the advancing tide of modern social life ; but his unique personality will be preserved by Miss Murfree's art, and will furnish one more picturesque element in the history of American life.

During the Civil War the Army of Northern Virginia was encamped for two winters not very far from the home of Thomas

Nelson Page, then a boy of eight years. On either side the plantation ran the two principal roads leading to Richmond, and it was known throughout the country-side that the army under Grant would probably pass that way when on its road to the Southern capital.

Much of the storm and stress of the actual struggle went on in this region, and the younger generation received an impression of the war only possible to eye-witnesses. Thomas Nelson Page was born of an old Virginia family which had been distinguished since colonial days. His great-grandfather on his father's side had been the friend of Thomas Jefferson and one of the leading patriots of the Revolution, while from his mother he was descended from General Thomas Nelson, one of the signers of the Declaration of Independence. The boy's own father was a major in the army of General Lee. As in many other Southern homes of the day, nearly every incident of life on the Page domain centred in some way around the war. The children knew little else besides the talk of battle and campaign, and they were so young that their memories hardly went back beyond the dark days in whose shadow they were living.

Young Page received thus in childhood those impressions which sank so indelibly in his mind that when revived in after-years they were still fresh and vivid. He knew all the discomfort that beset a neighborhood over which armies marched backward and forward, and he shared in the excitement which filled every heart when the news of Grant's advance was alternately reported and denied. Much of the actual horrors of war were also known by the boy, who became familiar with stories of defeat, of prison life, and of death, long before the age when children more happily placed learn of these things. These stories, told by fugitives, flying from the Northern Army, by soldiers home on furlough, or wounded and dying far from home, found their way to his ears and became a part of his life. It was natural that when he had become a man the memory of those childish days should prompt him to write

down some of the experiences which still lingered in his recollection.

His first published story, *Marse Chan*, was
written after reading a letter which had been
taken from the pocket of a dead Confederate
soldier. This letter, which was from the
soldier's sweetheart, expressed one of those
touching incidents furnished by the war, and
which Mr. Page used to such good effect that
the story is considered by some the best piece
of fiction born of the struggle.

The success of this story upon its appearance in the *Century Magazine* made its author
famous. He received letters from all over the
United States and from many places in Europe
congratulating him upon the pathetic and faithful picture he had drawn.

In this story the author struck a note which
vibrated with the tumult of the actual struggle
between North and South during the Civil
War. *Marse Chan* is the hero of the humble
negro who is made his chronicler, and the tale
is told with all the passion of hopeless sorrow.

In this story Mr. Page deviated somewhat

from the custom of other Southern writers. Their work mainly lay with the conditions preceding or following the war. But the author of *Marse Chan*, following the lines of his first story, has very largely chronicled the heart-history of the war itself. When, as in the case of *Marse Chan* and *Meh Lady*, the story is told by some faithful, devoted slave, the effect is indescribably pathetic. All the bitter feeling that raged between the two sections seems to fade away in the presence of a love so loyal and so unselfish.

Marse Chan was followed by other stories of equal interest, the series being embodied in book-form in 1887 and entitled *In Old Virginia*.

The next year appeared that charming little juvenile, *Two Little Confederates*, a story of pluck, adventure, and boyish heroism, for which the events of the war served as a background, and into which were woven many vivid pictures of the life of the period.

A series of essays—*The Old South*—still further vindicated Mr. Page's claim to recognition.

These essays, treating an old subject from a new
point of view, are full of that delightful color
which tinges all the author's work. They are,
moreover, examples of admirable workmanship, showing an artistic perception and a mastery of form.

On New Found River, Pastime Stories, together with other material not collected in
book-form, have, with their appearance, won
still higher fame for their author.

Since the publication of his first volume,
Flute and Violin, in 1891, James Lane Allen,
the historian of the blue-grass country, has continued to present, one after another, charming
pictures of his native State.

Flute and Violin is a story of the early days of
Kentucky, when the "dark and bloody ground"
was one of the outposts of American civilization. This little tale of two native musicians,
one an old parson and the other a lame boy,
shines with a tender light across the background
of bloodshed and ruin which darkened the early
annals of frontier life. Equally sweet and true

12

to the finer sides of life are the stories of *Sister Dolorosa* and the *White Cowl*, published in the same volume. In *A Kentucky Cardinal* and *In Arcadia* Mr. Allen has transcribed his love for nature into two pretty romances, he being a naturalist in the same degree that he is a novelist. His descriptions of Kentucky wild flowers, birds, fields, and roads are so true to nature that they might be inserted in treatises on natural science.

The literary world of to-day knows no voice truer and sweeter than that of this poet of his native fields and woods.

Among Southern writers in other fields Miss Grace King, Miss Sarah Eliott, Miss Molly Elliot Seawell, and others, following the lines of Southern thought, have presented its social life from many points of view. Thus expressed by the able and sympathetic artists, Southern fiction forms one of the most interesting movements of American literature.

CHAPTER XI

1833—1888

Louisa May Alcott, though born in Germantown, Pa., was by inheritance a child of New England, of which her father and mother were both natives. At the time of her birth her father had charge of a school, which, two years later, he gave up and returned to Boston, removing in turn to Concord when Louisa was eight years of age.

All the world has read in *Little Women* the chronicle of that happy childhood passed in the shadow of the Concord elms; and the experiences of the sisters Beth, Meg, Amy, and Jo, have won a place in American literature which the child-heart will never willingly let go. Undoubtedly the liveliest and brightest of the merry group of girls was Louisa herself, whose wit made stock out of household calamities, and whose ambition made defeat but an incentive to fresh endeavor. Two generations of children have now thrilled with delight over the recitals which have made that home-history, a great part of which is autobiographical, one of the most sympathetic revelations of childhood ever given to the world. For above and beyond the tale of merry adventure or mad escapade, there thrills that reminiscent quality to which the heart of childhood ever responds. Jo toiling from cellar to garret in her childish yet serious masquerade of Pilgrim's Progress, or Beth perplexed with tender pity over the mystery of death, are alike typical of the genuine thoughts of the child, and the youthful reader is often living over his own experiences when perusing this fascinating record. This unique charm, which is necessarily absent in great works of imagination, will no doubt give the story of Louisa Alcott's early days a permanent place in literature, as it has already accorded it a fame which rivals the classic renown of Robinson Crusoe and Robin Hood.

The happy life of the Alcott girls at Concord was shared by the children of Emerson, Hawthorne, Channing, and other prominent men of letters whose homes were then in that quiet village. Mr. Alcott was his children's teacher, and very often he was their most genial play-fellow. Their mother, a woman of noble nature and rare force of character, was their tender friend as well as their loving adviser. All the children kept diaries, and in Louisa's is recorded many of her struggles with a rather tempestuous nature, and many earnest resolves to be a " good child." Scattered here and there through the pages of the diary are found little notes from her mother, commending some special act of obedience or self-restraint, praises dear to the child's heart, whose highest ambition was to be dutiful.

To the Alcott children, books of course were familiar. Before she could read, Louisa played with books, building houses of histories and bridges of dictionaries. Even then she was possessed with a desire to write, and inscribed strange characters in the blank pages of Plutarch and Bacon. When the time for lessons and reading actually began, the children all became omnivorous readers, Louisa devouring novels, histories, poetry, and fairy stories with unappeasable appetite.

Being a New England child she was also taught to sew, becoming so skilful in this accomplishment that she set up a doll's dressmaking establishment, which became famous for its select styles, and was patronized by all the children in the neighborhood.

The Concord house had a large garden and barn attached, both of which were a delight to the children. In the garden their father gave them practical lessons in botany and in the study of nature, and in the barn they held meetings, discussed books, and acted plays. Once they found a little robin lying cold and starved on the garden-walk. They warmed and fed the pretty thing, and Louisa, full of tender pity, celebrated the event in her first poem, *The Robin*. The verses pleased her mother, whose praise was very sweet to the eight-year-old child. From this time she frequently wrote verses inspired by the circumstances of her childish life.   Her prose efforts were always more ambitious ; dramas and tales of heroic adventure were the only things thought worthy her pen, and the plays were undoubtedly a success.   They were acted in the barn, and for the time being the real Cinderella walked before the eyes of the audience, and the brave prince truly waked the Sleeping Beauty with a kiss.

By the time she was eleven years old Louisa, though so famous among the children of her set as an author of lively plays, was storing her mind with good literature.   She read Plutarch's lives and Scott's novels, Goldsmith, the life of Martin Luther, and the English poets outside the daily lessons, and the daily household tasks, for the Alcotts were poor, and the girls had each her special work.

Between eleven and fifteen Louisa passed the years at Fruitlands, a little settlement that Mr. Alcott had founded near Concord.   It was during this time that the children learned that in the coming years their mother must look to them for help in the support of the family, and bravely they set themselves to the task. Louisa in particular was inspired by a passion to be her mother's helper. Her whole soul was devoted to this object, and every scheme which presented itself to her mind had this end in view. For herself she cared as little as it was possible. One only little wish and ambition did she have, and that was to possess a little room of her very own where she might retire and "think her thoughts" without interruption, and do such work as came to her.

In one of those sweet correspondences which the old diary has preserved she confessed this desire to her mother. In an answering note we learn that the overworked and overworried mother found time and means somehow to accomplish this desire, and the little room, with work-basket and desk by the window, and a door that opened into the garden, made glad the heart of the unselfish child. About this time Emerson presented her with Goethe's *Correspondence with a Child*, a book that fired her imagination and introduced what she has termed the "romantic period" of her youth. She was fifteen, and it suddenly occurred to her that it would be an interesting thing to have such a friendship with Emerson as existed between Goethe and the child Bettina. She took to writing letters, which, however, were never sent; she wandered around by moonlight, and sat at midnight under the trees looking at the stars. Presently, however, her New England common-sense came to the rescue. She realized that her poetry was nonsense, and that she, in fact, had been very silly to try and worship as a romantic hero one whose friendship had from earliest years led her soul into noble paths.

When Louisa was eighteen her serious ambition was to write plays and become a successful actress. Her sisters had entire confidence in her ability to do both, and much labor was spent over the production and enacting of lurid dramas. It was a great event when the manager of a Boston theatre actually consented to bring out one of these plays, called *The Rival Prima Donnas*, although from some mistake of the management it was never produced. Later, a farce called *Nat Bachelor's Pleasure Trip* was produced at the Howard Athenæum and was fairly approved by the public and press.

During these early days of playwriting the Alcott girls were striving in every way to share the burden of the family expenses. Louisa sewed, taught, and wrote, but none of these things paid very well. The family poverty was a real and very distressing fact, and no way seemed to open toward a successful fight against it.

By the time she was twenty-two, however, Louisa had decided that her talent lay in the way of authorship. She at that time published her first book, a little volume of tales that she had written for Emerson's daughter Ellen, and which came out under the title, *Flower Fables*. This book contained some pretty fancies and showed some talent, but it is now only valuable as marking the beginning of a successful career.

Many short stories and poems had by this

time found their way to different papers and periodicals, and for the next seven years her pen was busy, though the remuneration she received was not entirely gratifying.

But the pleasure which this success brought was saddened by the fatal illness of " Beth," Louisa's favorite sister. After two years' suffering " Beth's " gentle spirit slipped away, leaving a place forever desolate in " Jo's " faithful heart. The old, revered friends, Emerson and Thoreau, helped to carry the little, worn-out body to its last resting-place in Sleepy Hollow, and Louisa wrote in her diary that she knew what death meant.

In 1861 Miss Alcott published her novel *Moods*, the most ambitious work she had yet attempted, and one on which she placed many fond hopes. But although *Moods* represented all the ideality and poetry of life as it then appeared to the young author, it was not a great success. She had toiled faithfully over its composition, and had wrought into it many of her own girlish dreams, but the heroine was not real, and many of the situations were artificial. The defect lay in the author's own gift, which did not reach out to work of a purely imaginative character.

Miss Alcott was bitterly disappointed over the meagre success of *Moods*, which she attributed to the many changes she had made in it, through the advice of the different publishers who had rejected it. In spite of the fame that her other books brought, *Moods* always held a warm place in her heart. Her true work for literature was indicated by an experience which widened her mind and expanded her sympathies as no girlish day-dreams could ever do. This was her life as a hospital nurse at the front during the early days of the Civil War.

The Alcotts had no sons to devote to the cause of the Union, but they sent their bravest and brightest one, the daughter whom the father so proudly called " Duty's faithful child," to serve her country in its hour of need. Miss Alcott was detailed to the Georgetown hospital, and here she entered heart and soul into her duties. The hospital was poorly equipped, and both patients and nurses suffered from bad air, impure water, and damp rooms, but all put thoughts of self in the background, and kept as cheery and bright as possible. The new nurse was a great favorite with the soldiers, who appreciated her fun and laughter, her un- failing devotion, and the womanly tenderness which never found her too tired to write mes- sages to their far-off friends.

Though often worn out, she never omitted her own home letters, which were faithful tran- scriptions of the daily hospital life. All its sad- ness and pathos appealed to her, and its humor- ous side, for it had one, found a response in her merry heart. Her experience here ended after six weeks, owing to a serious attack of typhoid fever. The bad air and drainage of the hospital had done their work, and Miss Alcott returned to Concord, where she was for many months an invalid. She never entirely recovered this shock to her health, and the invalidism from which she suffered in her last years in reality dated from this time.

Upon the suggestion of a friend she resolved to throw her experience at Georgetown into literary form, and wrote the first three of her *Hospital Sketches*. These immediately attracted so much attention that the series grew into a book which was published in 1865. This work, so full of real life, of the beauty of heroism, patience, and duty, brought Miss Alcott her first taste of fame. Eminent men, among them Charles Sumner, wrote congratulating her upon her success, and she found herself lionized by a public that was grateful for this glimpse of life at the front. About this time Miss Alcott published in the *Atlantic Monthly* her beautiful poem, *Thoreau's Flute*, a tribute to the character of that noble poet, and the most perfect piece of verse that the author ever made. A new and abridged edition of *Moods* appeared also, and owing to the popularity of *Hospital Sketches*, won a gratifying success. From this time Miss Alcott had no difficulty in finding a market for her wares. Her short stories and sketches were eagerly accepted by the best magazines and papers, and she even had some difficulty in keeping up with the demand for them.

In 1865 Miss Alcott made her first visit to Europe. She started as companion to an invalid lady, as her means did not allow her to make the trip otherwise, but later she joined her own friends and completed her visit in their company. This was a delightful experience, restful and health-giving to the hardworking author. It was her first real holiday and she enjoyed it with that fresh, buoyant spirit that was so characteristic of her. Upon her return a Boston publisher asked her for a book for girls, and from this demand, which she feared at first she could not comply with, grew her famous story *Little Women.* The full power and beauty of this story was unsuspected by the author, and she was dazzled by the brilliant success which followed.

Thinking that she was merely writing down the merry life of a happy family of girls, she was in reality making a transcription of typical New England girlhood, and putting the touches to a picture of rare value. All the best in New England blood and manners filters through the pages of this book. Pure living, noble thinking, high ideals here find a place and reflect the girlhood which was blessed by the friendship of Emerson, Hawthorne, Thoreau, and other of her father's associates, and which was guarded so tenderly by that father himself.

This book, which may be said to have heralded a new literature for children, was hailed with acclamation by the young audience for whom it was written. The publishers were busy keeping up the demand for the books, and Miss Alcott began to receive letters from all over the country demanding another volume. England, France, Holland, and Germany brought out rapid editions, and by the time the second volume was ready Miss Alcott's name was a household word wherever children read books.

This height, so unexpectedly but justly won, Miss Alcott never lost. For nearly twenty years longer the children of the land gave her the first place in their affections, while each successive book seemed to them a personal gift from the author. She was the friend and ideal of thousands of boys and girls who never saw her, but who felt, beyond a doubt, that their interests were known, and their hopes and ambitions dear to her. Far beyond what the author ever dreamed, these sweet and true stories of young life influenced the generation to which they appealed. Beyond what she had hoped, the little lessons of duty and noble living learned in the old house at Concord brought rich and noble harvest to far wider fields.

The home life of the family was at this time very happy. The eldest daughter, "Meg," was married and had two charming children, the "Demi" and "Daisy" of *Little Men*, though both babies were in reality boys. The youngest daughter, "Amy," was making progress in the study of art, and "Jo" herself was happy because she could earn money to make the others happy. Soon after the publication of *Little Women* she went abroad with her sister May, the "Amy" of *Little Women*, remaining four years; work as well as travel occupied the time. The day she arrived home her father

met her at the dock, with a red placard pinned
in the carriage window, announcing the publication of *Little Men*.   Like its forerunner, it
scored a great success.   The other numbers of
the *Little Women* series grew rapidly, *Old-
Fashioned Girl*, *Eight Cousins*, and *Rose in
Bloom* being perhaps the favorites next to the
initial volumes.   *The Spinning Wheel* series,
Aunt Jo's Scrap-Bag series, and *Lulu's Library*—three volumes for small children—appeared as the years went on.

Miss Alcott was also the author of a novel
called *A Modern Mephistopheles*, published
anonymously in the *No Name* series.   One of
her best-known books, *Work*, is founded on
the incidents of her own experience in her girlhood days, when money was scarce in the Alcott family, and the young daughters were
striving in every way to lift the burden from
father and mother.

Her sister May married and died abroad,
leaving her baby-girl to Miss Alcott, and to
this little niece she gave henceforth a mother's
love.   Her own mother and father were ever

her dearest care, and her greatest happiness lay in the knowledge that she had relieved their old age from want.

Miss Alcott died after a short illness in Boston in 1888.

Time had given to her the reward she would have chosen above all others—the knowledge that her work brought not only success, but that it carried its own message of life's great intention to each young heart that it reached.

CHAPTER XII

Thomas Bailey Aldrich, poet and novelist, was born at Portsmouth in 1836. Like many other New England seaports, Portsmouth, at the time of the poet's birth, had long ceased to be a wealthy and important town. No longer East India merchantmen, Mediterranean trading-vessels, English and French ships, or great whalers came up to its docks to leave their cargoes and sail away again to the distant lands whose names were so familiar to the inhabitants of the old town. That was the Portsmouth of the past which had shown such fine fighting qualities during the Revolution, and whose oldest inhabitants still remembered how their hardy little town did brave coast duty in the War of 1812. The Portsmouth of Aldrich's

youth was a quiet, sleepy place, which seemed
to be glad of a chance to spend its old age
quietly, and whose disused wharves and crumbling warehouses attested a long and honorable
career, though, like other earthly things, it had
come to an end.

In this quaint old town the better class still
dwelt in the family mansions built in the eigh-
teenth century; the fisher-folk lived in a separate part of the town, and they still flocked to
the wharves on the rare occasions of the appearance of a new sail in the harbor, in the
hope that here at last were tidings of some
husband or brother who had been lost sight of
for many a day. The actual interests of the
place still centred around the sea, though the
fleets which came in sight of the beautiful harbor, one of the finest in the world, seldom
dropped anchor there. But the atmosphere
was full of the romance and mystery of the
ocean. Old sailors who could tell tales of ship-
wreck and bold privateering still haunted the
wharves on sunny afternoons, and could be
found available for story-telling in their cosey

little cabins on stormy winter days. The expressions which the children heard in the streets, and often at home, in regard to the wealth, the local news, and world at large were often nautical relics of life on the quarter-deck riveted into the common New England speech. "Nor'easters" and "sea-fogs," "a squally fore-and-aft sky," and a proper lack of respect for longshoremen known as "butter-fingered land lubbers," were localisms familiar to all ears. The boys were all "messmates," and every one looked forward to owning a three-masted ship, for the sea, of course, was the only proper theatre of action for a Portsmouth boy.

Ardent lover of his native town as he grew to be, Aldrich in his very young childhood had a vague dream of Portsmouth and all the rest of New England as a barren waste inhabited by red Indians and poor-spirited whites who lived mainly in log huts. He imbibed this comical notion from a residence in New Orleans, whither he was taken while yet an infant, and where he lived for some years. In his charming *Story of a Bad Boy*, a biography of his childhood, he has told us how surprised he was to find that civilized and even respectable people lived at the North, his old nurse Chloe having always taught him that a " Yankee" was a being to be despised, utterly. Being taken to Portsmouth however to attend school, he soon became appreciative of the fine qualities of his stately white-haired grandfather, in whose family he lived, while his life at school opened up new vistas of delight. He had a very healthy and happy boyhood, many incidents of which are transcribed with grateful affection in the pages of the *Bad Boy*.

It is essentially the story of a New England boy of the generation which had escaped the sterner discipline of an older day. Still careful of the training of mind and character, the Puritanism of New England had in Aldrich's youth lost many of its unlovely characteristics. There was less gloom and formality, and, except in the observance of Sunday, many of the usages of early times had passed away.

Sunday was still, however, strictly kept. Aldrich gives an amusing description of that day on which his grandfather no longer appeared any relation to him, and when boyish sports, Robinson Crusoe and the Arabian Nights, were exchanged for three sermons a day and a visit to the family burying-ground.

With this exception, at school and at home, his life was full of healthful duties and pleasures. He describes particularly his delight in the first snow-storm which he saw in Portsmouth after his return from New Orleans, and how he stood by the window for hours watching the unfamiliar, beautiful scene. He made good progress at school, learning mathematics and Latin in the thorough New England fashion. He had a host of boy friends, as healthy and fortunate as himself. He was a prominent member of a flourishing secret society formed for the perpetration of dark and mysterious deeds; once he and the other members of the society cleaned some old rusty cannon which adorned the wharves, fired them off with a slow fuse at midnight, and awakened all the inhabitants under the impression that the town was being bombarded.

He owned a part of a boat and used to cruise among the islands off the harbor, and once he experienced the bitterness which many dwellers by the sea know, in seeing a young companion drift out forever from sight in the face of a great storm which destroyed twelve sail of an outgoing fishing-fleet before its fury abated.

Perhaps the dearest of his boyish treasures was his pony, Gypsy, who was "pretty and knew it, and passionately fond of dress;" who loved boys, and would have nothing to do with girls; who could " let down bars, lift up latches, draw bolts, and turn all sorts of buttons;" who once ate six custard pies that had been placed to cool, and enjoyed the wickedness of the feat as much as did her young master. She was an affectionate creature, too, and used to steal off whenever she could and go to the Temple grammar-school, which her master attended, and wait for him with her forefeet on the second step. Aldrich's first composition was devoted to the praise of the horse, a tribute to Gypsy, and when his school-days were over he

was only consoled at parting from her by his grandfather's solemn promise to sell her to a circus, for Gypsy had histrionic talent and could "waltz, fire a pistol, lie down dead, wink one eye," and do other tricks worthy of admiration. In her larger sphere she became the belle of the circus-ring, and performed wonders on the tan-bark.

When Aldrich was fifteen his father died suddenly in New Orleans. This changed the boy's life materially, as a college career had to be given up and some means of livelihood secured. At this juncture an uncle offered him a situation in his business-house in New York, and it was thought best that he should accept this position. In the last glimpse which he gives us of himself in the *Story of a Bad Boy* he says that his uncle insisted upon his taking the offer at once, being haunted by the dread that if left to himself the boy might turn out a poet.

This hint carries us to the beginning of Aldrich's literary career. As in the case of many other poets, this calling was not self-chosen.

The boy's ambition was to become a Harvard student, and it was only a sense of duty and an unselfish wish to save his grandfather further care that led him to consent to a business life. But in the end his choice wrought well for him. Denied the means of carrying on his studies as he would have liked, he became his own teacher. In the intervals of work he read and studied, and because he was a poet born he composed verses. Almost before he knew it this last occupation engrossed more and more of his time. The fancies which at first chased through his brain, the creatures of an hour's recreation, came at last to take up their abode there and to demand serious attention.

In this regard Aldrich's gift shows that it springs from true poetic inspiration. Even in his earliest verses there is evidence that behind the imagination and fancy lay the sense of the poet's mission to reveal in the form of art the beauty and harmony unseen by the common eye.

It is to be presumed that the young poet

kept these aspirations very carefully from
the knowledge of his uncle, who certainly
could find no fault with the manner in
which his nephew's office duties were performed.

By the time he was eighteen Aldrich had
prepared for the press a small volume of poems,
which he published under the title, *The Bells.*
Before he was nineteen he had written the *Ballad of Babie Bell,* that exquisite monody of
babyhood which brought him instant recognition as a poet of more than ordinary promise.
The *Ballad of Babie Bell* and other poems
appeared in book form in 1858. Aldrich
was then twenty-two years old. He had secured a position as publisher's reader, and
had contributed poems, essays, sketches, and
stories to *Putnam's,* the *Knickerbocker, Harper's,* and the *Atlantic Monthly.* In newspaper work he was connected with the New
York *Evening Mirror,* the *Home Journal,* the
Saturday Press, and other prominent newspapers of that date. The literary life lay before
him. Other volumes of poems were issued,

each showing the poet's true insight. From 1865 to 1874 he was editor of *Every Saturday*, and the following year he went abroad on a vacation justly earned.

He visited England and Ireland, France, Germany, Italy, and Austria. To each place he brought the sympathy of a finely attuned nature, and from each he seemed to carry away some experience that broadened his intellectual outlook. The itinerary of this journey was published afterward in the *Atlantic Monthly* in a charming series called *From Ponkapog to Pesth.*

Aldrich was later made editor of the *Atlantic Monthly*, a position which he held for a number of years. In American poetry this author has created a school of his own. The peculiar temper of his gift was shown in the *Ballad of Babie Bell*, in which the fragrant grace and innocence of babyhood seems to have been revealed to the poet in as pure a vision as ever came to a knight of the Holy Grail. This story of the death of a child, in which death is made so beautiful and childhood so holy, indicated that fineness of perception which is Aldrich's most striking characteristic.

All his conceits and fancies, his illustrations of life and character, both of his lighter and graver hours, reveal that delicate, inward vision which make his work so distinctive. His subjects are as varied as his own vagrant fancies, which seem to find all places in earth and air welcome and habitable. Sometimes it is a monk of the Middle Ages whose sin and repentance he incorporates in charming verse as in *Friar Jerome's Beautiful Book.* Again it is the old Hebrew story of *Judith*, or the Roman legend of *Ara-Cœli*, telling how the little waxen *bambino* found its way back alone in the storm and darkness to the convent from which it had been stolen.

An Indian maiden whose memory had become legendary long before the discovery of America; an old Greek coin bearing the coined head of Minerva; a castle of feudal days with arches crumbling to dust and drawbridge falling, each claims his fancy, and is by him woven into the graceful and beautiful fabric of his verse.

Nowhere is his touch more sensitive than in his appreciation of nature, as known to New England, where ice-storms and sleet and hail, fogs and bleak winds all become a part of the poet's consciousness and teach their own lessons of courage and endurance. New England wild flowers and summer fields have also their tribute from their own poet, who sings their praises in *The Blue Bells of New England* and who acknowledges no enchantment so binding as that of the May of his native land. *The Sisters' Tragedy* and the beautiful *Monody on the Death of Wendell Phillips* are also among the notable poems. *Wyndham Towers*, the most ambitious of the later poems, is a legend of the days of Elizabeth, which reappears in the reign of Charles the Second. This story of two courtiers of Elizabeth, who were brothers and rivals, and whose fate remained a mystery for over a century, is told by Aldrich in charming verse, characterized by his own peculiar graces of touch. *Unguarded Gates*, a collection of his latest poems, contains many beautiful specimens that reveal the master's mind, still alive to all those subtle varying moods of thought, which make his work so distinctive.

In prose Aldrich has produced more than one novel of character, true to the old New England traditions which moulded the thought of the Puritans, and artistic in execution. His prose, like his poetry, possesses the undefinable quality which sets it apart from other contemporary work. Among his novels, *Prudence Palfrey* and the *Stillwater Tragedy* are the best, while of his shorter stories, *Marjorie Daw* ranks easily first, both in point of literary excellence and from the will-o'-the-wisp remoteness which marks its relationship to the genuine fairy-brood.

In some ways the fancy of Aldrich very nearly approaches that of Hawthorne. Above all other New England writers these two possess the charm which unlocks that realm of fancy wherein wandered Spenser and Shakespeare, Shelley, Coleridge, and Keats. This wonder-world is not always open, even to poets;

whoever enters it must wear the badge of the elfin crew which wanders invisible at will, and which only kindred sight can discover. Aldrich, true knight of this goodly fellowship, has visited their haunts more than once. That he was well received is evinced by the secrets he has brought back and which he has woven with the poet's cunning into his art.

14

CHAPTER XIII

NEW ENGLAND WOMEN WRITERS

In New England, as well as in the South and West, the novelists of to-day have pressed their own surroundings into the service of art. The pictures they have given us are thus true to nature. They illustrate the quiet hours of the nation's life, the hours in which it truly grows and fulfils the purpose of its being, and the pictures are therefore very valuable. Most of this fiction is thrown into the form of short stories, and these are contributed by so many different authors that we are able to get many points of view.

The material here used is perhaps not so picturesque as that offered to the writers of the South and West ; New England, except in its earliest days, has never been the land of romance ; but here the progress of those ideas that make a country's greatness has gone

steadily on.   The writers of to-day still reflect
the thought and manners that were moulded
under the influence of the great men of the
past.   The genius of Hawthorne and the spirit
of Emerson made a permanent impression
upon American art and life, and the children
of their own blood have not forgotten their
lessons.   Thus we find New England fiction
largely dealing with the moral life of the people.   Character sketches, stories of temptation,
defeat and victory, battles lost and won by the
soul, form the *motifs* of these tales ; and although New England to-day can claim no
great novelist, yet its artistic purpose is as pure
and elevated as when it laid the foundations of
American literature.

Interwoven with these stories are many pictures of manners and home surroundings which
make an atmosphere of reality.   This atmosphere, changing with every age, as the conditions of life change, has been so reflected in
the work of to-day, as to make it in itself a
mirror of the every-day history of the people.
And this has its value also.

Perhaps the work of no woman writer so intimately connects the spirit of the New England of the past with that of to-day as does that of Mrs. Julia Ward Howe. Mrs. Howe has always been an advocate of ideas. Life has seemed to her a mission of service; although not a Puritan by descent, she has fought nobly in the cause of Puritanism, the cause of justice and humanity. Though her anti-slavery and philanthropic work, and her advocacy of woman suffrage have occupied much more of her time than her literary life, yet her writings belong eminently to the history of American literature. They represent very strongly the ideas which the republic has always sought to maintain, and in one case their author embodied in verse the spirit of the nation in one of its greatest hours. That poem, *The Battle Hymn of the Republic*, was a song and a prophecy of liberty in its highest sense. It was a reminder of the part that America had elected to play in the great drama of national life. Wherever its words fell they stirred the soul to such noble response, that it became the war-cry of the nation. It was sung in schools, and incorporated in the services of the Church; under its inspiration the Union forces marched on to victory, and the republic may be said to have achieved the great intention of its existence to the beat of its triumphant measures.

The air to which the song is set was heard originally in the South. A visitor from the North, present at a colored meeting, was struck by the vigor and swing which characterized the singing of this tune, and on his return wrote down the melody. The popular war song *John Brown's Body* was afterward written to this music. During a visit to Washington in the first year of the war, Mrs. Howe went one day to see a review of the troops; the drill was interrupted by a movement on the part of the enemy, and the sight of the troops filing back to cantonments fired Mrs. Howe's heart; she began singing *John Brown's Body* as the men marched past, and the inspiration of the *Battle Hymn of the Republic* came to her in that moment; the next morning at dawn she rose and wrote the words of the most famous song of the war.

Mrs. Howe was born in New York in 1819. Her father, Samuel Ward, was a man of wealth and prominent in public affairs. The family mansion near Bowling Green, then a fashionable neighborhood, was noted for its hospitality, and the children were accustomed to meeting the many famous men and women who found their way to New York. Julia was the fourth child, and was considered remarkably clever even in this family of bright children. She began to write poetry while still a very little girl, and since she was a born leader, she insisted that her younger sisters should also write poetry. Many childish scenes of despair occurred before this resolution was set aside, but Julia still retained her faculty for leadership. Whatever she believed was so vital to her that she seemed impelled to impress others with the same view. This characteristic, broadened and strengthened by favorable circumstances, enabled its possessor in later life to accomplish a noble work for humanity.

At the time of Mrs. Howe's childhood New York was the home of that brilliant circle of poets, essayists, and scholars who followed in the footsteps of Irving and made the culture of the day a noble foundation for its future literary life. Some of these men had been among the first Americans who made pilgrimages to the old world in search of the higher cultivated artistic life denied them at home. Many of them had given to European society its first glimpse of the best social life of the new world, and in more than one instance the nature and charm of their talents were appreciated abroad as well as at home. New York was still a small city. The fashionable streets were found in neighborhoods not far from the Battery, and the social life, though dignified, was in many respects very simple. Old-fashioned stages and family carriages were the means of conveyance beyond the city limits along the shady country roads which led toward Boston and Albany, and which are now known as the Bowery and the Western Boulevard. Much picturesqueness characterized the houses, many of which were built in the old Dutch fashion, and surrounded by large, luxuriant flower gardens. Christmas, Thanksgiving, the Fourth of July, and above all the Dutch New-Year's-Day, were still dignified festivals, honored and enjoyed by all classes alike.

In this atmosphere of ease and unostentatious wealth, of cultivation and thought, Julia Ward grew to womanhood. By the time she was seventeen she was an acceptable contributor to the leading magazines of the day, and at the time of her marriage with Dr. Howe, in her twenty-fourth year, she had laid the foundation of a successful literary career.

After a visit to Europe Dr. Howe and his wife, with their baby daughter, lived for a short time at the Institution for the Blind near Boston, of which Dr. Howe was director. Dr. Howe had already won fame for his successful attempt to educate the blind deaf-mute Laura Bridgman, and his noble work for the blind continued to engage his interest. He remained director of the institution all his life, residing for many years at a charming country place called "Green Peace." Mrs. Howe, from the time of her removal to Massachusetts, became identified with the political and social movements in which that State always led. One of her children speaks of her as having been a "Bostonian of the Bostonians," from the beginning of her married life. It is certain that her own nature responded warmly to the progressive New England spirit, and that her talents and earnestness won her a high place in the band of men and women who represented New England thought.

In 1853 Mrs. Howe published her first volume of poems under the title *Passion Flowers.* Although brought out anonymously the authorship was at once accorded to Mrs. Howe by Emerson, Longfellow, and other poets, who recognized in the verse her own fertile fancy. In the following year another volume, which was largely an appeal for the freedom of the Southern slaves, appeared under the title *Words for the Hour.*

From this moment Mrs. Howe's literary life became identified with the anti-slavery cause.

Poems, articles, editorials, and lectures all spoke the same word for humanity, and the author became known as one of the leaders in the cause. *The Battle Hymn of the Republic* only added another laurel to the fame she had already won as a tireless, fearless, and able advocate for the freedom of the slave.

When the war was over Mrs. Howe's pen still wrought for large issues. Well known as a lecturer, her efforts now were directed to questions of character, ethics, and the purpose of life. She was still a leader in the intellectual world, and the most eminent men of New England cherished her friendship.

Almost from the beginning of the movement Mrs. Howe has been a champion of the woman suffrage cause. She has been one of the workers who have done much for the broader education of women and opened to them wider spheres of usefulness. But her spirit is too large to be confined closely to one interest. The world has been her field of action, and whenever the word was needed there it has been spoken. In 1867, when the

Greek inhabitants of the island of Crete revolted from the Turkish Government, Mrs.
Howe and her husband crossed the Atlantic,
carrying money and supplies to the brave little
band of rebels. In 1872 she was in London
trying to bring about a woman's peace congress, having for its object the abolition of war
among civilized nations.

When the republic of Santo Domingo desired
to be annexed to the United States, Dr. Howe
was one of the commissioners appointed by
the United States to inquire into the feasibility
of the plan. Dr. and Mrs. Howe passed two
winters in the island, living at one time in one
of those large marble houses which the natives
call "palaces," and making journeys of inspection as to the wealth and resources of the
country. Their house was guarded by native
soldiers, and wherever they went the inhabitants vied with one another in offers of hospitality and friendship. It was Mrs. Howe who
revealed to these simple people to what stature
womanhood might grow. Her gracious influence seemed to represent to them the blessings

that might flow from a union with the great republic, and it was into her sympathetic ear they poured the story of their disappointment when their dream of a larger national life came to an end.

In later years Mrs. Howe's interests have been very closely connected with the New England Woman's Club, an outgrowth of her brain, devoted to the broader advancement of women. This last project connects her ideals closely with those of her young womanhood, when in all and above all she conceived life to be but the instrument for the working out of noble purposes.

Her place in American literature is representative. While the mass of her work is of necessity ephemeral, it is yet of invaluable character. Whenever, during her career, the nation has stood in danger from foes within or without, she has come to the front with her pen and the influence of her noble personality. So greatly has she wrought in this regard that the history of her literary career would be the history of the causes which have affected the national life for the last fifty years. No merely artistic gift, however great, could have won for her this place.

Louise Chandler Moulton, poet and prose writer, was born at Pomfret, Conn., in 1835. Around her childhood still lingered the traditions of old New England life, and her education was almost as strict as that of her Puritan ancestors. Louise was taught her catechism and the duty of going to church three times on Sunday, to do her little stint of sewing, and to listen respectfully while her great grandmother read her extracts from the Greek philosophers in the original. She was also taught that it was sinful to read novels and to dance, or to play backgammon. She was an only child, and as she had a loving little heart, the affection her parents lavished upon her made the home atmosphere most sweet and sunny. Like many another New England child she often forgot the terrors inspired by catechism and sermon to find pleasure in the world which she created out of her own

fancy. This world of imagination was in her
case peopled by creatures so real that they
formed an actual part of her life. Often the
same characters occupied her attention for
months, and she would hurry away from lesson
and task to live through hours of emotion and
experience with these children of her brain.
Once she spent a whole summer watching these
imaginary characters act what she called a
"Spanish drama." As soon as she appeared in
the garden they would flock around her and go
through the parts which they seemed themselves to create ; if they came to grief, she was
genuinely moved, and once, when one of them
died, she was utterly overcome. Outside these
fancies the voices of nature awakened many
curious thoughts.

The wind whistling through a certain key-
hole seemed to her distant bugle notes, or the
wailing of lost souls, while the tones of rain and
sleet had each alike its own weird interpretations. It is from such imaginative children
that the New England poets have sprung, and
when she was about seven years old the little

ʈ dreamer began to put her thoughts into
ʿse. Very curious bits of doggerel must
ʋe been the result of these moments of in-
ration, but they no doubt expressed in some
eer fashion the fancies teeming in the rest-
s little brain. When she was fifteen Louise's
ɪt printed verses appeared in a Norwich
wspaper, and three years later a volume enti-
d *This, That, and the Other*, appeared. In
s were included the stories, poems, and
ɛtches which had been printed in various
ɪgazines and papers, and which had won for
ɜ young author considerable reputation. The
ok was kindly reviewed by Edmund Clar-
ce Stedman and other critics, and the author
nost immediately took the position she has
ɪce held as one of the most sympathetic of
ew England writers. In her prose work
rs. Moulton has dealt with those studies
character which have such a charm for
ew England writers, and in the portrayal
which she has been strikingly successful.
er stories and novels have appeared in book
rm under the titles *This, That, and the*

Other, *Jono Clifford*, and *Some Women's Hearts.*

Some charming books for children, written primarily for the amusement of her own little daughter, show Mrs. Moulton's talent in another light. These tales—*Bedtime Stories; More Bedtime Stories; New Bedtime Stories*, and *Firelight Stories*—have won a wide hearing.

But it is by her poetry that Mrs. Moulton will be longest remembered. Her poems are full of melody, of light, and color; they are charged with an intense feeling for nature, whose moods they reproduce with exquisite fidelity; they are, in most instances, singularly perfect in form, while the beauty of certain single lines stands unchallenged. But above all they are the songs of one who sings spontaneously and naturally, to whom the outside world and the life of the soul have alike revealed themselves in music. In them is found the true expression of the author's gift as one of the best lyric poets of America. Some single poems, as *The House of Death; How*

Long; In Pace; and *Left Behind*, have won
a wide fame.   Her poetry has been published
in two volumes, *Swallow Flights*, and *Other
Poems.*

Another writer of the same generation as
Mrs. Moulton is Harriet Prescott Spofford,
daughter of Joseph N. Prescott, a descendant
of one of the families which have made New
England famous.   Miss Prescott's first work
marked her at once as a unique personality.
Hitherto the fiction of New England had been
stamped with a distinct moral purpose around
which the tale was woven.   But in the brilliant
and dramatic novels *Azarian, Sir Rohan's
Ghost, The Amber Gods,* and in the short
stories which belong to the same period, this
author seems to have created an art peculiarly
her own, for above all other things they appealed to the sense of beauty.   The language
in which they were written was new to readers
of fiction, and they were carried along by it
as by beautiful music.   This gift of expression,
chastened later to a severer beauty, so inten-

sified the charm of the story, itself always dramatic, that it seemed on first reading the
author must have sacrificed the purpose of the
true story-teller. But stripped of their luxurious dress the stories would still remain genuine experiences of life in New England, though
seen from a point of view seldom attained.
The poetic faculty so apparent in her prose
has made Mrs. Spofford's verse equally felici-
tous. Her mood in her earlier and perhaps
most successful work was an alien one to
New England fiction, full of a tropical beauty,
and dominated by a rare imaginative faculty,
and it will probably give her contributions a
permanent place among New England writers.

Elizabeth Stuart Phelps has, in her stories
and novels, dealt almost entirely with questions
of conscience and morality. She came of a line
of theologians whose lives were spent in discuss-
ing and teaching the principles of puritanism,
and much of their seriousness of purpose became her inheritance. Her first story appeared
in the *Youth's Companion* in 1857, before she

was fourteen, and five years later *Harper's Magazine* published her story, " A Sacrifice Consumed," one of the first stories called forth by the war. The year following she began writing the book which made her famous, and which appeared in 1868 under the title *The Gates Ajar*.

In this story the author, for the first time in American literature, showed how completely the old puritan idea of the hereafter had passed away. In its place had come a belief in the unfailing love of God, and a hope of the blessedness of the future life. The book brought comfort and help to thousands who had outgrown the gloomy creed of their ancestors, and whose hearts were still mourning the loss of friends who had fallen in the war.

But although the book achieved a remarkable success the author did not follow it with others of a similar character. She began instead the publication of a series of short stories dealing wholly with the problems of human life. Many of these stories are so sad, that they seem to show life only as a tragedy, but

the author's purpose was to preach the truth
in order that good might come of it. These
stories, published later under the title *Men,
Women, and Ghosts*, were followed by *The
Story of Avis*, a novel of remarkable force.
Like her other works, *The Story of Avis* is a
sermon thrown into the form of fiction, but
the artistic sense of the author is shown also
in this book as in no other. If Miss Phelps
had not written fiction she would still have
become a poet; few writers possess such insight, and fewer still are governed by the sense
of beauty that dominates all her work. Her
fiction is full of beautiful lines showing the
finest sense of color, while her volume of *Poetic Studies* illustrates how far her poetic instinct might have reached had her art been
confined to verse-making.

The Story of Avis is full of color and
rhythm, and is one of the best instances of
how far words may be made to reproduce the
lights and shades of the world of nature. These
two characteristics, the moral purpose and the
sense of beauty, have dominated all the au-

thor's works. Although her later works, *Dr. Zay*, *Beyond the Gates*, and others have been eminently successful, yet she reaches her highest point in such short stories as *A Madonna of the Tubs*, *The Lady of Shalott*, *Cloth of Gold*, and *Jack*. In these powerful tales, which read like poems, both characters and background are sketched in such fine lines as to place them among the best American fiction. The tragedy of common life which has always appealed to the author, and which has been her most successful theme, has never been more artistically treated. Miss Phelps was born in Boston, but her girlhood was spent in the old town of Andover, where her father was a professor of theology. She studied mathematics and the classics at the Andover Female Seminary, one of the celebrated schools of the day, and, like all the youth of her generation, she was taught that one of the chief duties of man was to brood over the theological problems that had puzzled her puritan ancestors. She has lived the greater part of her life in Andover. In 1888

she was married to the writer, Herbert D.
Ward.

Lingering to-day among old New England
villages and country sides are many characteristics of other days.   For, while society has
been progressive, the people have kept many
quaint habits of thought and speech, much in
the same manner as they have preserved in
their garrets the furniture and costumes of
their ancestors.   Thus, the men and women
found in village and farm-house seem often
survivals of another generation, and the story
of their simple lives is full of interest.   In
another generation, perhaps, these types will
have passed away, and the individuality which
has stamped New England life from its beginning will be lost.

Mary E. Wilkins has preserved in her
sketches of this life many of its unique characteristics, and has studied detail so carefully
that her work has a distinct value in the literature of American social life.

No feature in the apparently humdrum ex-

istence of these people has seemed to Miss
Wilkins uninteresting. She makes us sympathize with their little ambitions and humble
denials and sacrifices, until we feel we have
entered into close relationship with their lives.
We realize the misfortune of the poor old lady
who could not afford a front door, and see the
utter demoralization that follows when a lone
spinster loses her pet cat, her only companion
and friend. There is a sermon preached in
the story of the old woman who earned her
living by making patchwork quilts and who,
through a mistake, put the pieces that belonged to one neighbor into the quilt intended
for another. The author's gift, as a genuine
story-teller, makes the work alive with human
feeling, and gives to these uneventful tales the
charm of romance. Her power for present-
ing a picture is equally great. We see the old
farm-house kitchens, the sunniest and brightest
parts of the home, and have glimpses, much
like those that come to the occupants themselves, of the prim "front rooms" that are so
seldom used. We see, too, the orchards, mead-

ows, and fields rich with harvests or lying
bare under the winter skies; every detail of
farm and village life comes before us vividly
as if photographed; the farmer's wife busy in
the kitchen, the farmer himself sowing or har-
vesting, their son donning his Sunday clothes
for a visit to his sweetheart, or their daughter
up in her bedroom trying on the sheeny silk
which she is soon to wear as a bride, are all
careful copies of the originals whose personality supplies the human interest in these unique
surroundings.

From the first appearance of the stories in
various magazines and periodicals Miss Wilkins
was recognized as a writer whose work must
bear a permanent value. This New England
life, with its limitations and often unlovely
characteristics, was yet a survival of the old
puritanism, though the spirit of the past had
been in many instances subverted. Much of
the hardness and unresponsiveness of these
people were an inheritance as legitimate as
their stern sense of justice and love of truth.
Miss Wilkins, by seizing the salient points, has

given to their characters just that balance between the old and the new New England
which really exists, though time must speedily destroy it.

The short stories and sketches of Miss
Wilkins have been published in two volumes,
under the titles : *A Humble Romance* and *A
New England Nun*, each book taking its
name from the leading story. *A Humble
Romance* is, perhaps, the best of the short
stories. The descriptions of the tin pedler
vending his wares is like a scene from Dickens,
while the human interest of the story is traced
with the finest art.

Besides her short stories, Miss Wilkins has
published two novels, *Jane Field* and *Pem-
broke*, the first a charming love-story and the
second a tragic study of the unlovely side of
rustic character, relieved by the sweet and
steadfast faith of a young girl. Some charming stories for children show Miss Wilkins's
talent in a new light. Of these *Young Lucretia*, which gives the title to the book, is
a fair example of the author's insight into the

ambitions and interests of the child mind. Young Lucretia, who had never had a birthday or Christmas present, and who lives with some old aunts who have long since forgotten that they ever were children, is a quaint little picture of the old puritan up-bringing joined to the usages of modern life. We sympathize with the poor little heroine when she has to wear dresses made out of her aunts' cast-off garments, and we do not blame her for surreptitiously conveying some packages to the school-house Christmas-tree, so the children may not think she is utterly without presents. It was a sweet thought to leave the little maiden glowing in the happiness of a new-fashioned dress, with her heart throbbing over the thoughts of a real Christmas party, and with her two eyes " shining softly, like stars," as she gazes from the dusky fireplace into the face of the kindly visitor who has brought this gladness.

Among Miss Wilkins's other work she has given us one reflection from those dark days of the Salem witchcraft. This she has embod-

ied in her play, *Giles Corey, Yeoman*, in which
all the relentless spirit of persecution is
pitilessly portrayed. Giles Corey is a study,
full of dramatic force, and dominated by the
tragic elements that underlay many phases of
puritan character. Miss Wilkins has made in
this play another claim to her rank as the
greatest power in New England fiction to-day,
and as the author whose artistic realism em-
bodies the highest purpose of modern literary
art.

CHAPTER XIV

GEORGE W. CABLE

1844—

George W. Cable was born in New Orleans,
where his childhood, youth, and early manhood
were spent. The New Orleans of his childhood — a city of shrubs and flowering trees,
of vegetable gardens surrounded by palisade
fences, of handsome old-fashioned houses, un-
paved streets, and empty, marshy lots—is to
him a pleasant memory. Through the streets
he wandered, with his head full of day-dreams,
and when not busy with study or play, formulated a plan of life entirely different from that
he actually lived. A conscientious pupil and
omnivorous reader, his early ambitions were
still far away from such leanings ; long before
he had mastered his geography he had determined upon a career of adventure, and it was a

bitter disappointment to him to learn that his favorite romance, *Paul Jones, the Son of the Sea*, was not true. Yet even the names of foreign countries had a fascination for him, while the masts of the ships clustered at the docks were an inspiration. Even the ballast, which consisted sometimes of stone from Spain, had such an interest that it led to an attempt at studying geology.

Naturally the wharves had a great attraction for such a boy, and thither he used to go with his brother, day after day, to watch the vessels come in and depart, and to weave stories about their voyages. Once when a revenue cutter anchored across the river the two boys, though poor in pocket-money, paid their way over the ferry in order that they might sit down upon a stump of drift-wood and inspect her at leisure. Good fortune sent an official in their way, who, amused by their interest, invited them on board, and allowed them to inspect the various quarters, and to hover with delight over the sailors' lockers, where the thread, needles, and other outfittings suggested all the delights of sea life. The fact that he could not really travel turned his attention, perhaps, to the literature of travel and he began writing a story of two Spanish brothers who, in by-gone days, had made a voyage from Spain to the Caribbean Sea. This narrative was intended to embody all the wild and romantic tales that the young author had dreamed out, but only one chapter was ever written, though it was promised a place in a school paper of which Cable had been chosen editor—because he wrote a good hand. Much serious work went on hand in hand with these day-dreams and longings. Before he was ten he had read Hume's *History of England*, and had set to work to memorize the Declaration of Independence. At all times he would rather study than play, and Burns, Scott, Cooper, Shakespeare, and the Bible were read and re-read in the intervals of school work.

When he was fourteen his father died, and Cable was obliged to leave school and earn his living. He found employment in a customs warehouse, his special work being to put brands on the different articles. This prosaic work had, however, a certain charm for him, and as he marked the silks and spices from the East, the delft from Holland, olives from Spain, linens from England, and calicoes from France, he took many imaginary voyages to those countries. The interest of the student was still strong within him, and every possible opportunity for study was embraced.

When he was nineteen he entered the Fourth Mississippi Cavalry and served for the remainder of the war, carrying his Latin grammar and reader all through the campaign.

The war over Cable went back to commercial life; no idea of a literary career came to him, though from time to time he wrote newspaper articles upon various subjects, and at one time was a regular contributor to the New Orleans *Picayune*. But a student of the best fiction and of literary style, gifted with poetic imagination and an intense feeling for humanity, Cable found after a time the impulse for story-telling strong upon him. ·This was augmented by reading in some old news-

papers various accounts of the life of New
Orleans in its early days. The social life,
perhaps, of no other American city had so
picturesque a beginning. The old French families never became Americanized even after
the union of Louisiana with the United States.
They kept their family traditions and social
usages, regarding the Yankees who came to
make their home there as intruders. All the
old French love of gayety, of gentle breeding,
and of refined living made New Orleans a city
of which the social life was the leading feature.
The Creoles, the descendants of the early
French settlers, remained French for many
generations, even speaking English as foreign-
ers, long after Louisiana had begun to send
representatives to Congress.

Many charming episodes of this early life
were preserved in the old newspapers which
came into Cable's hands from time to time, and
inevitably the long past scenes were re-lived
in his imagination. Just as inevitably the time
came when certain incidents and characters
wove themselves so distinctly into stories that

they had to be written down, and when Cable had so transcribed three short stories his work as the portrayer of the old French life of Louisiana had begun.

One of these stories, *Sieur George*, was published in *Scribner's Monthly*. Being a venture into new fields its novelty no less than its art appealed to Northern readers, and when another story, *Jean-ah Poquelin* appeared some time later the author felt from the wealth of friendly criticism that his choice of material had been a wise one. Other stories were written, the series being published finally in a book called *Old Creole Days*. The success of this little volume showed how truly the author had entered into the spirit of those old days, which had become but a memory. His next work naturally dealt with the same period in a fuller and more picturesque degree.

Having in view a picture of strong lights and shadows, yet one true to life, Cable chose for his subject one of the old representative families of New Orleans, and throwing in as a background one of the many tragedies that

shadowed the history of slavery, he presented
a vivid and picturesque creation of historic
value. All the domestic and social events
which would go to make up the history of
a wealthy and influential Creole family were
pressed into service, while underneath ran,
like a moral, the reflected purpose of a life
far different from that of the present day.
Cable supplied the tragic element of this
novel in the story of the negro *Bras Coupé*,
who resisted authority because he had been a
chief in Africa and whose sad fate had been
discussed for generations around plantation
firesides. But this sombre side of the picture
was relieved by many charming episodes. All
the grace and exquisite gentleness of breeding
for which Creole men and women were celebrated, made this picture of old Creole life of
rare value. The Grandissimes, whose family
name gave the title to the book, became a familiar word as the story of their lives appeared
from month to month in the magazine through
which it was running as a serial. Although
The Grandissimes was a work of fiction, it

created an intense interest in the period which it described. Northern readers were especially charmed by a view of the luxurious and peaceful life that went on in Louisiana while the English Colonies were fighting the Indians, redeeming the soil, and finally winning their independence as a nation. During all this time the French in Louisiana, both on plantations and in cities, were reverencing their king, holding to the traditions of their ancestors, and opposing in the end as bitterly as possible the idea of annexation to the United States.

The Creoles were pleasure-lovers. · They had beautiful houses surrounded by large gardens, and their fête days were numerous and strictly observed. Much of their enjoyment was of the simplest kind. The birthday of a relative, or the christening of a child was made the occasion for a celebration to which all the many branches of the family were invited, and where merrymaking went on from morning till night. Many striking scenes in *The Grandissimes* illustrate this feature of Creole life. There is also obvious throughout the book, a

comical reflection of the resentment felt by
one member of the family, because France had
sold Louisiana to the United States. This individual, Raoul Innerarity by name, even went
so far as to paint a large picture showing
Louisiana, in the shape of a badly drawn female figure, "rif-using to hantre de h-Union."
Other touches throughout the book show the
feeling that existed, while many charming pictures of home-life abound.

The Grandissimes made Cable famous.
Although it elicited much adverse criticism
from readers who denied its truthfulness as a
picture of old Creole days, it yet must be
considered as one of the best works of fiction
produced by a Southern writer. It has been
followed by innumerable transcriptions of
Southern life from other hands, but to the
author of *The Grandissimes* must always remain the credit of being the pioneer in this
fascinating world of romance.

Mr. Cable's second book, *Dr. Sevier*, deals
with the period of the war, though it is not
a war story. The hero, Dr. Sevier, is a noble

character, whose forgetfulness of self and absorption in duty form the theme of the moral which runs through the book. A love-story, and the struggle of a man with misfortune, some echoes of war times, and many scenes of New Orleans life in 1863 and 64 are also woven into the story, which, although it lacks the picturesque charm of *The Grandissimes*, is yet valuable as a chronicle of many real events.

When England took Canada from France, and the Acadians were driven away from Nova Scotia by the English, they naturally sought refuge in the American colonies which still remained French. Many of them found homes in the West Indies, but many more fled to the lowlands of Louisiana, and gathering together friends and family formed themselves into little homesteads. Gradually a primitive agricultural community arose which differed in almost every respect from the plantation life of Louisiana, although the Acadians remained loyally French.

They were never very wealthy, they were seldom slave-owners, their wives and daughters still performed the household work, and their children, as a rule, could neither read nor write. But they had kept a certain simplicity of character and an ideal of life that made them in the main truthful, loving, and self-respecting. Sometimes their little villages dotted the prairie lands, joining one another by straggling houses and homesteads along the high roads. Sometimes they gathered in little hamlets along the outskirts of the great plantations, the men and women earning their livelihood in the cotton and sugar fields. Very often they were found in the swamp lands and cities adapting themselves to new conditions. But always they remained separate in habit and life from the Creole.

To one of these little Acadian settlements which had grown up on the Louisiana prairies Mr. Cable went for the inspiration of his third novel, *Bonaventure*. The hero, Bonaventure, was an orphan boy who was being brought up by the village curé. This old priest, pious, loving, and beneficent, saw in Bonaventure a soul that would be sure to work largely for good or

evil, and he watched over the child with zeal-
ous care. The story tells how Bonaventure,
in the first trial of his life yielded to temptation, how he repented and by self-sacrifice
wrought out his punishment, and how he finally became the great hope of the Acadians by
becoming a teacher and bringing to their children the gift of education. The story has
three divisions, the separate scenes of which illustrate the life of the prairies, the plantations,
and the swamps of Louisiana. In each the
local color is true and effective, the scenes and
incidents being in many instances studies
which the author made while visiting the regions as an official of the government.

This little story, in which the Acadian was
introduced into literature for the first time
since the publication of Longfellow's *Evange-
line*, shows Mr. Cable at his best as a story-
teller pure and simple. One of his most
successful books, it is also one in which he
has incorporated most conspicuously his own
large faith in the possibility for good which lies
in every human soul.

During the production of these three novels Mr. Cable had also been busy at other literary work. Much of this has been devoted to a study of Louisiana and New Orleans from a historical point of view. Searching among old records and historical documents, newspapers, and Government reports, he sifted out the material for a series of brilliant articles, since published in book form under the title, *The Creoles of Louisiana.* Here he pictured the growth and life of the old colony, in poetic yet truthful words, which made the record read like romance, although it was genuine history. Other historical articles, as *New Orleans Before the Capture,* and some Encyclopædia articles, further illustrate the author's power for picturesque effect in dealing with facts, while his *Strange True Stories of Louisiana,* edited from original documents, show how well his art can make truth reveal itself in all the fascinating colors of romance. *Madame Delphine,* another story of creole life; and *John March, Southerner,* a story of the time immediately following the Civil War, and the scene of which is laid partly in the South and partly in the North, completes the list of Mr. Cable's novels.

His work, which first revealed the possibilities for literature that lay in the old-time Southern life, created a new field in American fiction. Not only are his stories valuable reminiscences of other days, but they are full of an uplifting faith in man and in the power of goodness to adjust the many evils that deface human institutions.

Outside of his other literary work, Mr. Cable has been an aggressive worker in the field of practical politics, writing many essays upon the questions which affect the state and municipal government of the Southern States. He is also well known as a lecturer and critic upon literary art, and in recent years he has become one of the most popular platform readers, commanding large audiences wherever he appeared.

His home has been for many years at Northampton, Mass., from which place as a centre he directs many interests outside his own life. Among these may be included a number of Home Culture Clubs, which bring him into touch with thousands to whom his help and advice are an inspiration.

CHAPTER XV

JOHN FISKE

1842—

In history and philosophy the work of the past generation of American writers has been supplemented by that of John Fiske, an original thinker whose writings reveal much of the vital significance of scientific thought.

John Fiske was born at Middletown, Conn., where he lived during boyhood. His grandfather's home, in which he was bred, was a typical New England household, and he was carefully trained in all the precepts of good conduct. One of his first memories dates from the time when he listened gravely to the discussions that were frequent in the home on religion, politics, and morals. From these conversations it was, perhaps, that he very early pondered over questions of right and wrong, and settled the pres-

tige of all the kings and queens of the world—
which he had learned in chronological order—by
classifying them as " good " or " bad." When
moral questions became too hard for him to
decide he would refer them to some older head,
being firm in the conviction that grown people
knew everything. Thus he once astonished
the cook by asking her if Heliogabalus was
good or bad, and he not infrequently puzzled
other people by his persistent effort after information.

Fiske cannot remember when he learned to
read, but he was studying Latin at six, and at
seven was reading Cæsar. *Goldsmith's History of Greece*, and the *History of the Jews*, by
Josephus, were read before he was nine years
old, with the whole of Shakespeare, some parts
of *Paradise Lost*, and *Bunyan's · Pilgrim's
Progress*, the last a special delight because
here were argued those questions of right and
wrong which always fascinated him.

Notwithstanding this serious bent of his
mind Fiske had a healthy boy's love of play
and out-of-door life. And in this New Eng-

land home he had also certain duties which he performed faithfully. Apart from his love of reading, and his faculty for asking startling questions, he seemed on the outside an ordinary boy. Yet from his earliest years he was a thinker. Just as Emerson in his boyhood pondered over the meaning and uses of life, so Fiske puzzled over moral questions and the duty of man to the race.

Side by side with this seriousness lay his inexhaustible thirst for knowledge. To satisfy this he read and re-read every book that he could lay hold of. History especially delighted him. By the time he was eleven he knew his Froissart as only such a boy could. In the lively company of that goodly poet he visited the court of Edward III. and saw the tournaments and pageants, the knightly deeds and historic spectacles of the age of chivalry. Feudal castles, royal hunts, the clang of armor, and the shouts of battle filled eye and ear while he wandered through those fascinating pages, though outside the snow might be lying on quiet New England fields, or the sun shining on scenes so commonplace that they seemed part of another world.

With equal delight he followed Gibbon through his story of the fall of Rome, once the mistress of the world, and whose armies and law-makers had moulded the modern nations out of the savages who lived on the banks of the Seine, the Rhone, and the Thames.

The works of Robertson and Prescott were also a never-ending source of pleasure. Some idea of the extent of his general reading may be gathered from the fact that at this time he compiled from memory a chronological table extending from the age of Homer to the year 1820, and filling sixty pages of a large blank-book.

Two years later he studied men from Horace and Sallust, Cicero and Juvenal, and other Latin writers, and as he had been studying Greek for four years he began a course of the Greek philosophers, poets, and historians.

In the meantime there came a desire to write. By the time he was fourteen this had formulated itself into the intention to write a work on the philosophy of history. This idea did not seem in the least unusual, to him, and he was puzzled to find that the minister, to whom he confided his plan, did not sympathize with him as enthusiastically as he had expected. Soon after this Fiske began a course of scientific study, taking up geology, zoölogy, botany, and kindred subjects. By the time he was ready to enter Harvard he had also taken a course in mathematics, had studied navigation and surveying, was reading French, Italian, and Portuguese, and keeping his diary in Spanish.

Few young men could boast of such a mental equipment as Fiske's when he entered Harvard in his nineteenth year. But great as was the knowledge he had absorbed from books, the development of his mind had been still greater. Although in the main unconscious of it, he had become a profound thinker; while engaged in tracing the world's intellectual progress through ancient and modern times he had gathered the self-poise, and command of material which made him, later, one of the intellectual forces of his generation.

While at Harvard Fiske took a two-years'
law course, intending to practise for a living;
but he had been moulding his life on other
lines, and he found it impossible to ignore this
fact. Every detail of a lawyer's business was
distasteful to him, and after a short trial he
gave up his office and turned to the literary life.
He had already become known as a writer for
reviews and other periodicals, and although his
friends thought it unwise for him to place
dependence upon literature, his success soon
proved that his choice had been a wise one.

In nearly every case Fiske's books have been
the outgrowth of lectures delivered in colleges
and other educational institutions, or in public
halls. His work has been on two distinct lines,
history and philosophy; in the first he now
stands as an acknowledged authority; in the
second he is known as a brilliant expositor of
Spencer and Darwin, and as a thinker who has
himself made a distinct contribution to the
theory of evolution.

In one of his early books, *Myths and Myth
Makers*, Fiske relaxed somewhat from his

severer studies to trace in some charming
chapters the history of various popular superstitions and legends. While the book shows
the hand of the scholar, it also shows the light
fancy which he could bring to play upon his
subject; the gift of the story-teller is apparent here, as many of the fairy stories which
charm children to-day are traced back to an
origin older than the first records of written
history. In pleasant fashion we are here taught
that many popular heroes who have figured in
the folk-lore of England, France, Germany,
and other countries, were, after all, but wandering free lances, whose real home was far away
in Asia, in those fertile table-lands where man
first learned to till the soil and raise herds.
When that old Aryan race, the mother of the
greater part of the world to-day, began to
migrate it carried along with it those heroes.
Since that time they have been veritable gyp-
sies, taking up their abode here, there, and
everywhere, but keeping always close to their
blood relations, so that whoever hears the
story of their adventures knows that the
17

writer is of the old mother - race, and that
he is but retelling the tales that his kindred
have listened to for thousands of years.

Fiske's most important historical work is his
Discovery of America. In the intervals of
other work he was for a period of thirty years
going over the ground necessary to the accomplishment of this great task.

Beginning with Ancient America, he traced
the history and achievements of the tribes
which existed ages ago on the American Continent, and whose ruined temples, fortifications,
and dwellings were a marvel to the European
discoverers. The author's wide knowledge of
universal history and of prehistoric times enabled him to illuminate his work with many
pictures of wonderful interest. Thus in describing the Eskimo, probably the first white
race of America, he brings in also the story
of the cave-dwellers of Europe, from whom the
Eskimo are supposed to be descended. In
doing this he presents a vivid picture of those
curious people who lived in caves above the
shores of inland lakes, who hunted the mam-

moth and mastodon, and left behind them many carefully drawn sketches of their warriors and hunters.

These chapters are followed by others of equal interest, in which we trace the story of the ancient Mexicans and Peruvians, of the Pueblo Indians, and the tribes of the plains; then we have accounts of the old stories which claim that the Chinese were the first discoverers of America, these being followed by the tales of the Irish adventurers, and of the vikings. There is also a summary of the fanciful stories which floated over Europe long before the days of Columbus, in which philosophers, travellers, poets, and witches alike prophesied the existence of another continent far beyond the confines of the Western Sea. We have also a description of the state of Europe during this time when men were searching for Cathay and its inexhaustible mines of wealth, or carrying on the Crusades, or searching for the Indies over new routes, on which they supposed—if the world were round—they would have to sail uphill and down-hill to reach the other side.

With the same fertility of resource the story is carried down through the voyages of Columbus and the other explorers, the conquest of Peru and Mexico, and the colonization of the New World and its subsequent history until 1806, when Lewis and Clarke crossed the Rocky Mountains by following Indian trails, to survey the new territory just bought from France by the Government of the United States. This work, which is in reality a summary of the world's progress in scientific thought, shows the author's conception of the sphere of historical writing. There is a mastery of detail which makes it an invaluable guide for the student, and a philosophical breadth that is equally instructive to those who like to trace the events of history to their moral sources.

Another valuable work is the *Beginnings of New England*, which was elaborated from a course of lectures delivered at Washington University, St. Louis. This book has a peculiar interest for American literature, as it contains a history of the growth of the idea of popular government from the earliest times to the verge of the American Revolution. Comparing the rule of the ancient world with that of the modern, the author shows how the idea of popular government first arose, how it took root in the Anglo-Saxon race, formed the charter of English liberty, and finally was embodied in distinct form in the English colonies of the New World. The story of the Puritan settlement of New England, of the warfare with the Indians, the founding of Harvard College, and the growth of civil institutions, is followed by a recital of the troubles with the mother country, the tyranny of Andros and his overthrow as the last royal governor. This work, dominated by Fiske's masterly style, forms a preface to the *American Revolution*, a brilliant and learned history of the causes that led to the revolt, and in a series of luminous pictures takes us successively through the scenes of the French Alliance, Valley Forge, the war on the frontier and ocean, the treason of Arnold, and the final victory at Yorktown. Some of the finest ex-

amples of the author's work as a literary artist
are found in this book. He shows here, too,
that genius for characterization which marks
the true historian. Nowhere in historical composition are shown more striking descriptive
powers than where he draws the comparison
between the character of Benedict Arnold and
the common soldier of the Revolution, who
held the honor of his country sacred, and who
counted personal loss as nothing in the accomplishment of a holy trust.

The Critical Period of American History
follows naturally, taking up the period from
the end of the Revolution to the inauguration
of Washington. The Revolution had left the
colonies free from British rule, but there was
still no bond of union between them. Each
State was independent of every other, and it
seemed for a time that although they had
fought side by side for freedom, jealousies and
misunderstandings would now keep them far
apart. The wisest men of the age saw the need
of a general government to which all should be
equally bound, and for many years their efforts

were directed toward this end. Fiske relates the story of this critical period, during which it seemed sometimes that the States were drifting toward anarchy, so impossible was it for them to decide upon a concerted plan of action. Finally, however, after a succession of leagues, conventions, and federations, the States, one by one, accepted the Constitution as it was laid before the Legislature of Pennsylvania by Franklin, and the United States took their place as a nation. This work is one of the most important contributions ever made to the history of the United States, and, like the author's other work, it is dignified in diction, lucid in style, and abounds with a wealth of material that makes it serve as a text-book for the student as well as a volume for the general reader.

In American Political Ideas Fiske traces the growth of American political life from the primitive town-meeting of the early settlers to the rise of great civil institutions. The book has a particular interest as showing how the Anglo-Saxon race through all its wanderings has still kept to its early traditions.

Apart from his historical work the genius of Fiske has found its best expression in his philosophical writings. His *Cosmic Philosophy*, the earliest of his philosophical works, embodied the discoveries of Darwin and the other great evolutionists. In this as in all his works Fiske has consistently persevered in preaching the doctrine that moral ideas underlie all great scientific discoveries, and that evolution is the means used to develop the race spiritually. In his *Destiny of Man* and *The Idea of God*, this idea is illustrated by arguments so forcible, and by so clear an insight, as to give the author high rank as a teacher of spiritual truths.

CHAPTER XVI

MARK TWAIN
(Samuel L. Clemens)

1835—

Among the writers who have added greatly to American literature by transcribing the humor that lies in the American nature, the one who has won distinction under the pen name of Mark Twain perhaps ranks first.

Samuel L. Clemens was born in Florida, Mo., in 1835, but while very young his family removed to Hannibal, on the banks of the Mississippi, where his childhood was spent. The Hannibal of that day was a typical river town of the West, whose existence depended upon the traffic brought to it by the passage of the steamboats up and down the Mississippi. This river was then the great highway between the States of the Middle West and New Or-

leans, the depôt to which was taken much of
the produce from the farms and plantations
along its banks. All the towns and villages
along the Mississippi, from New Orleans up-
ward for hundreds of miles, depended largely
upon the river for means of communication
with the rest of the world; the flat - boats,
keel-boats, rafts, and steamers that passed in
endless succession up and down were, as a rule,
manned by men from the river towns, and it
was the height of every boy's ambition to be
a steamboat captain, or failing that, a pilot,
deck-hand, or even cabin-boy.

In his book *Life on the Mississippi* Mark
Twain has given us a sketch of the typical boy
of his early days, who only knew real happiness during the short time occupied by the lad-
ing and unlading of the freight from the two
steamboats that passed daily by Hannibal. He
says that the town was really awake only during these two intervals, and that after the last
boat had steamed away again, Hannibal went
to sleep and slept until time for the appearance
of the next day's boat.

Like the other boys of the village, Samuel
Clemens desired above all other things to be a
pilot on one of the steamers that plied between St. Louis and New Orleans. But as
his family objected to this occupation for him
he was apprenticed, at the age of thirteen, to
a printer; after learning his trade he visited
various cities and worked at the printer's case
in St. Louis, Cincinnati, Philadelphia, New
York, and many smaller towns. But dissatis-
fied with this life he finally returned West and
fulfilled the ambition of his boyhood by becoming a pilot on the Mississippi.

Life on the Mississippi is full of the detail
that characterized the lives of the boatmen of
that day, and it contains, besides, many picturesque illustrations of a phase of American
society that was confined to that period and
place alone.

It is therefore a genuine bit of local history
from the pen of a native historian, and it has
its own place in any study of American social
life. Not the least amusing and interesting of
these sketches is the one describing what a

river pilot had to learn in the days of Mr. Clemens's youth.

The boys of Hannibal had supposed that the least intelligent of them could readily learn to be a pilot in a few hours—it seemed so easy just to steer in and out of the docks, to keep clear of other boats, and to guide up or down mid-stream. But the youthful adventurer who actually stood beside the pilot at the wheel, taking his first lesson in river navigation, found that learning to steer was not so easy.

Mark Twain says that the pilot on his boat was expected to know every bend and point on the Mississippi River for fifteen hundred miles and how they looked in daylight, at dusk, and at night; how their shapes might change as the river twisted and turned; how they looked when the shadows hung around them on moonlit nights; how to tell them from the shadows themselves, and how to feel their presence when the blackness was so great that no man could see anything a yard ahead. The pilot was also supposed to know the depth

and width of the river at every point; to be
acquainted with every rock, snag, and bar, isl-
and, and reach ; to know every plantation between St. Louis and New Orleans, and thus
be able to land any travelling planter at his
own door.   But intricate as this knowledge
seemed, Mark Twain was able at last to
master it, and he became one of the best
pilots on the river.   He was able also to store
his mind full of pictures of river life, and
when he reproduced them many years afterward in *Life on the Mississippi*, the reader
was able to see again the busy life of those
long past days. ' Incorporated into the pilot's
story are also many interesting accounts of incidents and persons in some way identified
with the region.   The visit of Charles Dickens and of Mrs. Trollope, an account of the
Mardi Gras, some old Indian legends, and a
visit to Mr. Cable, who had just published
The Grandissimes, brings the narrative down
to the present day and summarizes the development of that part of the West and South.

In his twenty-sixth year Mark Twain ceased

to be a pilot, and for the next few years became a wanderer, visiting Nevada, California,
and other Western States, the Sandwich Islands,
and finally New York, where he published his
first book under the name that has won him
fame, and which was taken from the old river
measurement, "Mark twain." The principal
story of this first book, *The Jumping Frog
and Other Stories*, had previously appeared
in a newspaper, and with the other sketches
had won for the author some reputation.
He had during his travels been clerk, newspaper reporter, editor, and lecturer, being
sometimes successful and often unsuccessful.
Now, with a desire to see more of life he sailed
for Europe. Two years later appeared an account of his European journey in the book entitled *The Innocents Abroad*. It was this book
which in a few months made the author famous
wherever the English language was spoken.
Professedly a book of travel it was in reality
a burlesque on books of travel. From first to
last the pages were full of comical descriptions
of all that travellers had hitherto revered.

Historical cities, palaces, museums, works of art, even the very rivers and mountains that had helped to make history were by this irreverent scribe made to take on lights and colors so humorous that it seemed as if the author had discovered a new Europe. *The Innocents Abroad* experienced a success accorded to few books. It had an immense sale, and so universal was the appreciation of it that even the mention of the author's name would evoke a smile. In his next two books, *Roughing It* and *The Gilded Age*, Mr. Clemens portrayed American life on the plains, and as represented by the character of Colonel Sellers, one of those impractical enthusiasts whose schemes for making money without work forms the background for a character sketch so vivid that, thrown into dramatic form, it has proved one of the most successful of modern plays of its class.

But Mark Twain's love of humor and his indescribable faculty for seeing the funny side of everything are closely balanced by his power as a student of human nature and by his genius for the pathetic. His first works be-

longed strictly to the domain of humorous
literature, but his later work has shown the
serious side of his nature and his attainment
both as a student of books and of men. A
striking example of this is found in some of his
juvenile works where are strongly seen the tender sympathy of the man with all the impractical and romantic schemes of boyhood, and the
fine vision which sees in the ambition of the
child the impulse that often leads to noble
manhood.

In one of these juveniles, *The Adventures
of Huckleberry Finn*, the author has taken for
his hero a typical boy who belonged to Hannibal as it was in Mr. Clemens's youth. This
boy is made to do all the things that the young
Samuel Clemens and his friends wanted to do
and could not. He runs away from home,
lives on the Mississippi for days on a raft, and
has all the adventures that were dreamed of by
the boys whose horizon was bounded by the
great river that was at once their pride and
their despair. *Huckleberry Finn*, outside its
romance, is also a careful study of types that

abounded in the West. Negro dialect and backwoods speech, the manners of the river boatmen and the customs of the lower class of Missouri landsmen, are all woven into the story with the nicest art and serve to make it a delineation of high artistic value.

In another book, *Tom Sawyer*, Huckleberry Finn appears as the friend of the hero, and hand in hand these two boys walk through the pages of an ideal boys' book, one in which pluck, manliness, and heroism form the motive for the action, at once simple, natural, and sincere. These two books, with *Life on the Mississippi*, are studies that American literature is much the richer for. They are distinct from other sketches of social life in dealing with a class that had hitherto been unchronicled, and they place the author among the valued contributors to the history of American social customs.

A book that departs entirely from this view of life is *The Prince and the Pauper*, a study of life in the days of the young King Edward VI. of England. In this book Mr. Clemens

18

takes for his theme a subject which he says
may be history, or only legend or tradition, and
adds that the events chronicled may have happened or may not have happened, but at any
rate they could have happened. Thereupon
he spins a pretty story about Edward VI. and
the little pauper, Tom Canty, who by the
simple expedient of exchanging clothes with
each other set the whole kingdom by the ears
and nearly lost Edward his crown.

Many pictures out of English history are
woven into this story in a way that shows
the careful research of the student. London
in the early part of the sixteenth century,
with its palaces and wretched beggars' hovels,
with its famous Tower full of prisoners of
noble birth, and its military parades and street
fights between apprentices and serving-men,
passes before the eye like a panorama, while
the picture of the little king, who, clothed in
rags and mistaken for a beggar, still de-
mands homage from every one, is startlingly
true to the age when royalty was considered a
divine right and the king's person a sacred

thing. The story, which takes the unhappy
Edward over many rough ways and in much
strange company, in which he travels with beggars, thieves, and outcasts, is full of many
pathetic incidents which illustrate the society
of the day. A few brief descriptions here and
there show the author at his best as a lover
of his kind and the possessor of broad and noble sympathies.

Another book of which old English scenes
form the inspiration is *A Connecticut Yankee
in King Arthur's Court.* Here the author
takes for his hero a typical Connecticut Yankee of the nineteenth century, and transports
him back to the days of the Round Table.
The hero's adventures with King Arthur and
Lancelot, his contempt for the usages of chivalry, and his disgust at the ignorance of the
knights of the Round Table, are amusingly
detailed by the hero himself, who by his knowledge of modern science outdoes the magic of
Merlin, introduces telephones and bicycles into
the country, starts factories, schools, and poly-
technic institutions, and is only kept from mak-

ing a modern nation of ancient Britain by the
discovery that the people themselves do not
want these changes, that they are content with
their own ignorance and Merlin's magic, and
that progress, as known to Yankeeland, is a
thing they will have nothing of.

Pudd'n - Head Wilson is another story of
American life strong in conception and vig-
orous in handling. In some ways this book
shows Mark Twain at his highest point, as the
keen observer and critic who can read the emotions of the soul and out of the study build up
one of those characters in whose delineation
modern fiction is so successful. *Tom Sawyer*,
the boy, and *Pudd'n-Head Wilson*, the man,
alike belong to the American novels that will
live. In these, as in all his later work, though
the humor is always present it is the graver
side of life that claims attention and shows the
author as the careful student of character.

Mark Twain's latest book, *The Personal
Recollections of Joan of Arc*, is a beautiful
chronicle of the brave maid of Orleans whose
story has touched the world for hundreds of

years. Mr. Clemens spent a year in Paris getting material for this work ; he became a frequenter of libraries and a student of old records and memoirs, pursuing his study with all the zeal of the historian. His industry was rewarded by the production of a beautiful historical romance, in which the character of Joan shines fair and true amid the actual surroundings that girt her short life. Nowhere in his work is more apparent his reverence for womanhood and his appreciation of fine character than in this tender portrait of the young girl whose tragic fate he made his theme.

Mr. Clemens's home is in Hartford, Conn., where he has lived for many years. Outside his literary career he is known as a lecturer of singular success, and within and far beyond the home circle he is cherished for those fine graces of character and that sympathetically affectionate nature which have won him innumerable friends.

Printed in the United States
140341LV00009B/64/A